Doing a
SYSTEMATIC
REVIEW

A STUDENT'S GUIDE

Edited by

Angela Boland, M. Gemma Cherry & Rumona Dickson

Los Angeles | London | New Delhi
Singapore | Washington DC

Los Angeles | London | New Delhi
Singapore | Washington DC

SAGE Publications Ltd
1 Oliver's Yard
55 City Road
London EC1Y 1SP

SAGE Publications Inc.
2455 Teller Road
Thousand Oaks, California 91320

SAGE Publications India Pvt Ltd
B 1/I 1 Mohan Cooperative Industrial Area
Mathura Road
New Delhi 110 044

SAGE Publications Asia-Pacific Pte Ltd
3 Church Street
#10-04 Samsung Hub
Singapore 049483

Editor: Katie Metzler
Production editor: Thea Watson
Copyeditor: Neil Dowden
Proofreader: Elaine Leek
Indexer: Bill Farrington
Marketing manager: Sally Ransom
Cover design: Francis Kenney
Typeset by: C&M Digitals (P) Ltd, Chennai, India
Printed in Great Britain by
CPI Group (UK) Ltd, Croydon, CR0 4YY

© Angela Boland, M. Gemma Cherry and
Rumona Dickson 2014

Chapter 1 © Rumona Dickson, M. Gemma Cherry and
Angela Boland 2014
Chapter 2 © M. Gemma Cherry and Rumona Dickson 2014
Chapter 3 © Yenal Dundar and Nigel Fleeman 2014
Chapter 4 © Janette Greenhalgh and Tamara Brown 2014
Chapter 5 © Nigel Fleeman and Yenal Dundar 2014
Chapter 6 © Michaela Blundell 2014
Chapter 7 © M. Gemma Cherry 2014
Chapter 8 © M. Gemma Cherry, Elizabeth Perkins,
Rumona Dickson and Angela Boland 2014
Chapter 9 © Angela Boland, Sophie Beale and M. Gemma
Cherry 2014
Chapter 10 © Gerlinde Pilkington and
Juliet Hockenhull 2014

First published 2014

Library of Congress Control Number: 2013949489

British Library Cataloguing in Publication data

A catalogue record for this book is available from
the British Library

ISBN 978-1-4462-6967-1
ISBN 978-1-4462-6968-8 (pbk)

Doing a

SYSTEMATIC

Contents

Figures

Tables

Boxes

About the Editors

This book is the result of the collaboration of researchers who are linked to the Liverpool Reviews and Implementation Group (LRiG). This research group was established in 2001 and the major focus of their work is related to conducting systematic reviews of clinical and cost-effectiveness evidence. Members of the group also have experience in supporting students who are conducting systematic reviews as a part of their academic endeavors.

Dr. Angela Boland has worked at LRiG since it was established in 2001. During this time she has carried out many systematic reviews of both clinical effectiveness and cost effectiveness of health care interventions. As Associate Director of LRiG, she has also managed and proof-read many others. She has a Master's degree and PhD in Health Economics and an undergraduate degree in Economics and Spanish.

Dr. M. Gemma Cherry is a trainee clinical psychologist at the University of Liverpool. Prior to commencing training, she worked at LRiG for several years, conducting systematic reviews particularly in the field of psychology. She has an undergraduate degree in Psychology from Newcastle University and a PhD in Medical Education from the University of Liverpool. Gemma is a strong believer in evidence-based practice and that empirical research should be underpinned by systematic reviews.

Professor Rumona Dickson has been involved in the conduct of systematic reviews in health care for over 20 years and has been the Director of LRiG since 2001. During that time she has also been involved in a number of Master's programs that have promoted the use of systematic reviews as a learning tool to help students better understand the role of research in the evolution of health policy and practice. It is these experiences that prompted her to convince her colleagues to contribute to this book.

About the Contributors

Ms. Sophie Beale joined LR*i*G in 2011 after having spent 11 years at the University of York carrying out economic evaluations and service reviews in a range of treatment areas for pharmaceutical, NHS and government clients. Her main role within LR*i*G is to contribute to analyses of the cost effectiveness of new pharmaceutical products and she also enjoys contributing to other types of studies when time allows. Sophie has just started a PhD at the University of Liverpool.

Ms. Michaela Blundell has worked as a statistician at the University of Liverpool since 2009. During that time she has developed her skills in meta-analysis methods and has worked on a number of systematic reviews of health care interventions. She has a Master's degree in Statistics from Lancaster University and an undergraduate degree in Psychology and Statistics from the University of Liverpool.

Dr. Tamara Brown has worked as a systematic reviewer since 2001. Tamara worked at LR*i*G from 2009 to 2012 and is now at the University of Edinburgh. She has conducted a number of systematic reviews on behalf of the UK Health Technology Assessment Programme and for the Cochrane Collaboration. She has also contributed to National Institute for Health and Care Excellence (NICE) guidance. Her main areas of research are in Public Health, specifically the prevention of obesity and smoking. Tamara has a PhD by completed work based on a series of publications of systematic reviews of interventions to treat and prevent obesity.

Dr. Yenal Dundar has worked as a researcher conducting systematic reviews on a wide range of topics in health care since 2001. During that time he has developed skills in the area of systematic identification of evidence, which is an essential step in the systematic review process. Yenal is a former GP, and is working in the NHS as a Consultant Psychiatrist. He was awarded an MPhil from the Faculty of Medicine, University of Liverpool in 2006,

Membership of the Royal College of Psychiatrists in 2010 and the Certificate of Completion of Training in General Psychiatry in 2013.

Mr. Nigel Fleeman has been a researcher at the University of Liverpool since November 1994. Originally working in Public Health, he conducted a number of relatively short primary and secondary research projects for local NHS bodies before he joined LRiG in October 2006. Much of his work since has been to conduct systematic reviews of the clinical effectiveness of both medicines (mostly, but not limited to, cancer drugs) and pharmacogenetic tests on behalf of the UK Health Technology Assessment Programme. Nigel has a Master's degree in Public Health from the University of Liverpool.

Dr. Janette Greenhalgh has worked as a systematic reviewer at LRiG since October 2006. During that time she has conducted a number of systematic reviews on behalf of the UK Health Technology Assessment Programme and also for the Cochrane Collaboration on a wide variety of topics including cardiovascular disease, lung cancer, sickle cell disease and epilepsy. Janette has a PhD in Psychology from Bangor University and a PGCE in Adult Education from Llanddrillo College.

Ms. Juliet Hockenhull began working at LRiG in 2005 as a clinical reviewer working on both single technology assessments for NICE and health technology assessments for the Health Technology Assessment Programme. In addition, Juliet carried out large-scale updates of systematic reviews of prevention and intervention strategies, and of risk assessment tools for populations at high risk of engaging in violent behavior. As a consequence of these updates, Juliet has registered for a PhD and aims to devise and evaluate a clinical decision support tool that will assist clinicians when choosing interventions to reduce violence in adults with learning disabilities.

Professor Elizabeth Perkins is Director of the Health and Community Care Research Unit (HaCCRU) and William Rathbone VI Chair of Community Nursing Research at the University of Liverpool. She has spent 20 years undertaking research studies in the field of health and social care policy. Before working at the University of Liverpool, Elizabeth worked at the Policy Studies Institute undertaking large-scale surveys and small-scale in-depth qualitative studies for a range of funders including the Department of Health. She took up the post of the Director of HaCCRU in 1997 and has since specialized in undertaking qualitative studies, often using grounded theory, in the fields of mental health, aging and addiction.

Mrs. Gerlinde Pilkington has been working as a researcher with LR*i*G since 2009 despite her background being rooted in History and Classics. She works on systematic reviews covering a wide range of topics, and really enjoys the challenges and diversity each project brings, from mental health to cancer treatments. Gerlinde has also contributed to the organization and delivery of systematic review teaching workshops.

Foreword

Conducting a systematic review is a daunting challenge – despite the common ground offered by the review process, each review is slightly different. If we visualize the review as a journey, a common analogy, we need to share such a journey with a reassuring companion equipped with local knowledge and a plentiful supply of experiences. This book is such a companion, assembled by a well-regarded and experienced team from one of the UK's reputed national systematic review centres and packed to the brim with their distilled know-how.

As the authors acknowledge, there are many 'How to do it' books on the market. So why should a postgraduate student choose this particular companion for this challenging journey? For such a journey you want a companion who knows what they are talking about – whether embarking on focusing the question, searching or summarizing the data, the team speaks with a collective and authoritative voice. The chapters are liberally populated with frequently asked questions and, even for a seasoned traveller like myself, there are sufficient well-constructed travel tips to make this an essential guide. You also need a well-mapped route and, no doubt, you will find the trail signposted by the book's ten chapters as easy to follow as anything even remotely comparable. Furthermore you don't want to spend such a significant period of time trapped with a bore, and the entertaining and engaging style used to illuminate this book will ensure that your journey will pass speedily and enjoyably.

My bookshelves are already laden with 'How to do it' books on systematic reviews – very few of these are readable, informative and useful. But what do I do when I need to inform tomorrow's supervision meeting? Quite simply – I reach for this book!

Andrew Booth
Reader in Evidence Based Information Practice
School of Health and Related Research (ScHARR)
University of Sheffield

Preface

Why did we write this book?

There are a variety of excellent books written by systematic review experts that provide the 'How to...' of carrying out a systematic review. Why, then, did we think it was necessary to write a new one for students? Well, we wrote this book for two reasons.

First, we have long held a strong conviction that carrying out a systematic review as a postgraduate research project can yield excellent learning opportunities for students. Increasingly, academic and scientific communities are also acknowledging the value of this research activity. Reviewing requires insight into the fundamentals of research. Students learn to develop research questions, critique research findings and, most importantly, synthesize findings and make recommendations regarding how to use results in professional practice. These are valuable skills for students to learn, no matter their academic or professional discipline.

Second, we wanted to reflect on the systematic review process from the viewpoint of a student working independently (most likely at Master's level, but perhaps at PhD level) undertaking a systematic review as part of their academic program. Even though the 'How to...' books are useful to students, they frequently don't focus on the 'But what do I do when...?' type questions that so often arise during the review process. These are the questions that students need to know the answers to more or less immediately so that they can move forward with their theses. Whilst our book provides a comprehensive guide to carrying out a systematic review, it focuses more on the *practicalities* of systematic reviewing rather than the theory underpinning it. This book is for students who are carrying out a systematic review, not simply learning about them.

The book contains ten chapters. The first provides background explaining why systematic reviews are important, how they came about and why they provide an excellent learning opportunity for students. The remaining nine chapters focus on the actual systematic review process and offer methodological and practical advice on conducting and reporting this type of research within the format of a postgraduate thesis. Each chapter ends with a 'Frequently Asked Questions' section. These questions have been taken from actual student supervision meetings and highlight the most common challenges encountered during the review process. They include not only the 'What do I do?' type questions but also the 'Why do I do this?' and the 'What are my options?' type questions. Our answers set out practical approaches to help students deal with these issues. We've also designed a website (www.liv.ac.uk/systematic-review-guide) which contains resources to complement the material in this book; any student can browse our online systematic review materials and search for information that is relevant to their own review.

We have drawn on our own experiences of carrying out systematic reviews; all of the authors have worked with or in LR*i*G for a number of years. This means that the focus of the book is on the systematic review of health care interventions using quantitative methods. The target audience for this book is postgraduate students and we suggest approaches that encourage students to tailor review questions and review methods to meet their own specific learning objectives. The book is written by researchers with experience in the field of health studies, but it is also relevant to students in other disciplines, such as social work or education, where there is encouragement to systematically review current research or practice. However, we know that there is more than quantitative data to review so we have included introductions to reviewing qualitative data and health economics data, both of which are currently exciting, controversial and evolving areas of research. We acknowledge that these two sections only offer students a starting point.

What does this book have to offer you?

We had to make some general assumptions regarding the typical reader of this book. We thought long and hard about the research skills and resources postgraduate students might have at this point in their academic journey. Based on this, we have assumed that you, the typical reader of this book, will:

- be carrying out a systematic review as part of postgraduate study;
- have access to a computer;
- be able to search the Internet;

- have word processing skills and not be afraid to use them;
- have your own learning objectives relating to either professional practice or to the research process;
- have a specific research area in mind;
- be working (mainly) independently;
- need to meet a set-in-stone deadline.

We've tried to make the contents of this book useful and easy to read. We've assumed that you want a no-frills approach and each chapter is written with this in mind. The basics of systematic review methods are delivered in bite-sized chunks so that you are not overwhelmed by the enormity of your project. Students tell us that they are happiest (and most productive) when they are in control of their own research and are not relying on others for data or direction. This book is therefore written to guide you as you take control of your review. We are confident that it will help you move forward at your own pace. We know that you will want to excel in your studies so we have set out at the end of each chapter what an examiner might be looking for in the final thesis.

Future partnerships

We do not see publication of this book as the end of our work with students; we see it as the beginning of a partnership. We plan to build on the educational resources we have brought together in this book and add to those we've provided on our website. We'll use our materials to continue to support students who are interested in the rewards of systematic review methodology. We therefore encourage you to submit questions to us via our website (www.liv.ac.uk/systematic-review-guide) and we look forward to hearing from you about your experiences as systematic reviewers.

1

Carrying Out a Systematic Review as a Master's Thesis

Rumona Dickson, M. Gemma Cherry and Angela Boland

guide
supervisor studies outcomes
searches methods economics
protocol research systematic
practical
meta-analysis quantitative
synthesis discussion databases management
FAQ student post-graduate
question qualitative searching review
quality-assessment data
thesis

> **This chapter will help you to:**
>
> - understand the term 'systematic review';
> - gain an awareness of the historical context and development of systematic reviewing;
> - appreciate the learning experience provided by conducting a systematic review;
> - become familiar with the methods involved in carrying out a systematic review.

Introduction

In this chapter we introduce you to the concept of systematically reviewing literature. First, we discuss what systematic reviews are and why we think carrying out a systematic review is a great learning experience. Second, we give you an overview of the evolution of systematic review methodology. Third, we introduce the key steps in the systematic review process and signpost where in the book these are discussed. Finally, we highlight how systematic reviews differ from other types of literature reviews. By the end of the chapter we hope that you will be confident that you have made the right decision to carry out a systematic review and that you are looking forward to starting your research.

What is a systematic review?

A systematic review is a literature review that is designed to *locate*, *appraise* and *synthesize* the best available evidence relating to a specific research question to provide *informative* and *evidence-based* answers. This information can then be combined with professional judgment to make decisions about how to deliver interventions or to make changes to policy.

Systematic reviews are considered the best ('gold standard') way to synthesize the findings of several studies investigating the same questions, whether from health, education or other disciplines. Systematic reviews follow well-defined and transparent steps and always require the following: definition of the question or problem, identification and critical assessment of the available evidence, synthesis of the findings and the drawing of relevant conclusions.

A systematic review: a research option for postgraduate students

As a postgraduate student you may be offered the choice of conducting a primary study (for example, a cross-sectional survey) or a secondary research project (for example, a systematic review) as part of your academic accreditation. There are very good reasons why you are asked to carry out a research project as part of your studies, the most important being that *doing* a research project enables you to both understand the research process and gain research skills.

Systematically reviewing the literature has been accepted as a legitimate research methodology since the early 1990s. Many Master's programs offer instruction in systematic review methods and encourage students to conduct systematic reviews as part of postgraduate study and assessment. It is widely acknowledged that this approach to research allows students to gain an understanding of different research methods and develop skills in identifying, appraising and synthesizing research findings.

Every Master's course and every academic institution is different. For you, this means that the presentation of your thesis as part of postgraduate study must be carried out within the accepted guidelines of the department or university where it is due to be submitted. Your thesis must be an independent and self-directed piece of academic work; it should offer detailed and original arguments in the exploration of a specific research question and it should offer clarity as to how the research question was addressed. Conducting a systematic review offers you the opportunity to showcase your skills both as a reviewer and as a researcher.

Let's assume that you are interested in studying issues related to unintended teenage pregnancy. As a researcher, you have a variety of investigational methods open to you. However, the likelihood of being able to pursue these may be impeded by time and resource constraints, as well as by the specific requirements of your academic institution. Table 1.1 illustrates a number of possible project options open to you and the likelihood of you being able to successfully complete your chosen project as part of your postgraduate thesis.

In our experience, students who opt for primary research will mainly explore questions relating to current status and/or correlation factors; the main problem with this kind of research is that its generalizability is often hampered by small sample sizes and time constraints. However, students who

Table 1.1   Example project options for postgraduate students interested in unintended teenage pregnancy

Question	Research options	Type of research	Risk* of not being able to complete this as a Master's student
Relationship questions			
What is the incidence of unintended teenage pregnancy in my practice or region?	Epidemiological survey	Primary	Low
What programs are available in my practice or region for reducing teenage pregnancy rates?	Survey	Primary	Low
What are the most commonly reported methods being used to decrease rates of teenage pregnancy?	Systematic review	Secondary	Low
Correlation questions			
Is there a relationship between education levels and rates of teenage pregnancy in my practice or region?	Survey of existing data	Primary	Moderate
What are pregnant teenagers' views on the importance of sex education?	Focus groups or structured interviews	Primary	Low, with small sample size
What is the reported relationship between education level and rates of teenage pregnancy?	Systematic review	Secondary	Low
Causation questions			
Will the provision of emergency contraception in schools decrease teenage pregnancy rates?	Intervention study	Primary	High
What impact do one-to-one counselling and group meetings have on rates of abortion for teenagers experiencing unintended pregnancy?	Randomized controlled trial	Primary	Very high
What have been shown to be the most effective programs for decreasing teenage pregnancy rates?	Systematic review	Secondary	Low
Qualitative questions			
What are the views of teenagers on the reasons for high teenage pregnancy rates?	Focus groups	Primary	Low, with small sample size
What are the reported views of teenagers on the reasons for high teenage pregnancy rates?	Systematic review	Secondary	Low

* Low = you are in control or have unlimited access to the data that you need; moderate = you may or may not have to go through an ethics committee, you are dependent on other people to give you data or you need to recruit participants; high = your study is likely to be expensive, time consuming and/or dependent on the interest of others.

form questions to be addressed using systematic review methodology have the opportunity to work with a variety of different study designs and populations without necessarily needing to worry about the issues commonly faced by researchers carrying out large-scale primary research. Due to the very nature of a systematic review, students are able to work in the realm of existing research findings whilst developing critical appraisal and research synthesis skills. A systematic review provides an excellent learning opportunity and allows students to identify and set their own learning objectives.

Good research is rarely carried out on an ad hoc basis. From the outset, you need to be clear about why you are carrying out your systematic review. For example, you may want to evaluate the current state of knowledge or belief about a particular topic of interest, contribute to the development of specific theories or the establishment of a new evidence base and/or make recommendations for future research (or you might just want to carry out your review as quickly and as effortlessly as possible to gain your qualification). However, you need to think about what you want to learn from your systematic review. You might find that balancing your learning objectives with the objectives of the review may be challenging at times; this is most likely to be true if you are reviewing a topic of interest in your professional field (as we suggest you do). Discussing your learning objectives with your supervisor and exploring alternatives with your classmates or colleagues can often help you to clarify these objectives. Box 1.1 outlines some of the advantages and disadvantages relating to conducting a systematic review as part of a Master's thesis.

Box 1.1

A systematic review as a Master's thesis: advantages and disadvantages

Advantages:

- You are in control of your learning objectives and your project;
- You can focus on something you're interested in;
- You don't have to gain formal ethical approval before you begin;
- You don't have to recruit participants;
- You can gain understanding of a number of different research methodologies;
- You can gain insight into the strengths and limitations of published research;

- You can develop your critical appraisal skills;
- The research can fit in, and around, your family (or social) life.

Disadvantages:

- You don't experience writing and defending an ethics application;
- It can be isolating as you will be primarily working on your own;
- You don't face the challenges of recruiting participants;
- You may not get a sense of the topic area in terms of lived experience;
- You are reliant on the quality and quantity of available published information to address your research question;
- You may find the process dull or boring at times;
- There are no short cuts and the process is time consuming.

Evolution of the systematic review process

There are some common misconceptions about systematic reviewing. Some students (and supervisors) choose empirical projects over systematic reviews because they worry that systematic reviews aren't 'proper research', or that systematic reviews can only be conducted in the field of health. If you are thinking of conducting a systematic review as part of your Master's thesis, then we think that it will set your mind at ease to know a little bit about the history and evolution of the systematic review process and the disciplines to which systematic reviews apply.

It might surprise you to know that the systematic review of published evidence is not new. As early as 1753 James Lind brought together the data relating to the prevention of scurvy experienced by sailors. He wrote:

> As it is no easy matter to root out prejudices … it became requisite to exhibit a full and impartial view of what had hitherto been published on the scurvy … by which the sources of these mistakes may be detected. Indeed, before the subject could be set in a clear and proper light, it was necessary to remove a great deal of rubbish. (Chalmers, Hedges and Cooper, 2002, p. 14)

From Lind's farsightedness we move to the 1970s. Two important events took place that laid the foundations for a revolution in the way that evidence could be used to inform practice in health care and other areas. In the UK, a tuberculosis specialist named Archie Cochrane had recognized that health care resources would always be finite. To maximize health benefits, Cochrane proposed that any form of health care used in the UK National Health Service (NHS) must be properly evaluated and shown to be clinically effective before use (Cochrane, 1972). He stressed the importance of using evidence from randomized controlled trials (RCTs) to inform the allocation of scarce health care resources. At about the same time, in the USA, work by Gene Glass (1976) had led to the development of statistical procedures for combining the results of independent studies. The term 'meta-analysis' was formally coined to refer to the statistical combination of data from individual studies to draw practical conclusions about clinical effectiveness. In years to come, outputs of both research communities would combine to form the basic tenets of systematic review methodology. In 1979 Archie Cochrane lamented:

> It is surely a great criticism of our profession that we have not organized a critical summary, by specialty or subspecialty, adapted periodically, of all relevant randomized controlled trials. (Cochrane, 1979, pp. 1–11)

In response, a group of UK clinicians working in perinatal medicine made every effort to identify all RCTs related to pregnancy and childbirth. They categorized the studies that they found and then synthesized the evidence from these studies. This work led to the development of the Oxford Database of Perinatal Trials (Chalmers et al., 1986). In addition, their ground-breaking work was published in a two-volume book which detailed the systematic and transparent methods that they had used to search and report the results of all relevant studies (Chalmers, Enkin and Keirse, 1989). This work was instrumental in laying the foundations for significant developments in systematic review methodology, including the establishment of the Cochrane Collaboration in 1992. The Cochrane Collaboration is an international network of more than 28,000 dedicated people from over 100 countries who work together to help health care providers, policy makers, and patients and their advocates and carers make well-informed decisions about health care. They do so by preparing, updating and promoting the systematic reviews that they conduct, which are known as Cochrane Reviews (The Cochrane Collaboration, 2012). Since the development of the Cochrane Collaboration, others have followed suit. The Campbell Collaboration was established in 2000 and is focused on reviewing literature to demonstrate the effects of social interventions, particularly in the areas of education, crime and justice (The Campbell Collaboration, 2012). More recently, the Department for International Development (DfID) has used the results of systematic reviews to develop national and international policy in many countries worldwide (Department for International Development, 2012).

Why all the fuss? Why have people spent so much time developing a systematic review process? The answer is quite simple. Given the amount, and complexity, of available information and the limitations of time, there has been a real need to develop and establish a process to provide, in a concise way, the results of research findings. Most notably, the dramatic increase in the amount of accessible research today makes it impossible for decision makers, policy makers and professionals to keep up to date with advances in their field. Systematic reviews allow concise synthesis of a large body of research and therefore address some of these issues.

Why are we telling you all of this? Well, there are two important points to take away from this historical background. First, we want to convince you that *systematic review methodology is accepted as a research methodology in its own right*; in light of this, we use the terms 'review question' and 'research question' interchangeably throughout the book. In fact, most funding bodies require a systematic review of the literature to be performed before they will fund an empirical research project. In the UK, systematic reviews form the basis for the National Institute for Health and Care Excellence (NICE) guidelines for treatment and clinical practice. Throughout the world Cochrane Collaboration and Campbell Collaboration systematic reviews are viewed as the gold standard in this type of research. Literature reviews are also an integral component of any doctoral thesis. Whilst you wouldn't necessarily be expected to produce a review as detailed or as comprehensive as a Cochrane or Campbell review for your thesis, if you follow the systematic review methodology outlined in this book, then you can be confident that not only are you conducting research, you are producing some of the highest quality research possible.

Second, we want to show you that although the systematic review process began, and is common, in the field of health care, *systematic reviews are being carried out and used to inform decision making in a variety of disciplines and professions*. In fact, if you conduct a quick Internet search combining the terms 'systematic review' with 'education', 'social work', 'veterinary medicine' and so on, you can see for yourself the widespread application of systematic review methodology. Irrespective of the field in which you study, the basic tenets of systematically reviewing the evidence are the same. When researchers or practitioners are faced with a problem, they aim to identify, assess and bring together the evidence relating to that problem. This information can then be used to inform changes to policy and/or professional practice.

What are the basic steps in the systematic review process and how can this book help me to follow them?

There are nine basic steps to be taken when carrying out a systematic review. These are presented in Box 1.2 along with signposts to the chapter(s) of this book in which they are discussed in more detail. These steps are continually referred to and explored throughout this book, so don't worry if you don't recognize all of the terms at this stage. A good-quality systematic review will transparently report all of the steps that have been carried out so that the reader has sufficient information to be able to replicate the review. Additionally, providing details about each step makes it easy for the reader to assess the validity of the review's findings. The remaining chapters of this book provide you with a pragmatic, yet detailed, approach to carrying out each of these steps and we focus our attention on research activities that are essential to the successful completion of your review as part of a postgraduate thesis.

┐ **Box 1.2** ┌

Nine steps in the systematic review process

Step 1: Performing scoping searches, identifying the review question and writing your protocol (Chapter 2)

In this step you carry out scoping searches to help you identify background literature which will help you to define and refine your review question and set your inclusion criteria. You will also write a protocol. The protocol is a written plan ('map' of your journey) that enables you to set out the approach you will use to answer the review question.

Step 2: Literature searching (Chapter 3)

The aim of this step is to identify papers (published and unpublished), using bibliographic databases and other evidence sources, which address your review question.

Step 3: Screening titles and abstracts (Chapter 3)

In this step you read the titles and abstracts of the studies identified by your searches and discard the ones that aren't at all relevant to your review question and keep the ones that may be relevant.

Step 4: Obtaining papers (Chapter 3)

This step involves obtaining the full-text papers of the evidence that you identified in Step 3.

Step 5: Selecting full-text papers (Chapter 3)

This is when you apply your inclusion criteria to your full-text papers and ruthlessly exclude ones that don't fit the criteria.

Step 6: Quality assessment (Chapter 4)

In this step you assess each included full-text paper for methodological quality using an appropriate quality assessment tool.

Step 7: Data extraction (Chapter 5)

This is when you identify the data you require from each paper and summarize these data in tables.

Step 8: Analysis and synthesis (Chapters 5, 6, 8 and 9)

This is where you scrutinize and synthesize your data, either narratively or through meta-analysis. We discuss how to do this step in Chapter 5 (if you want to undertake a narrative synthesis) and Chapter 6 (for those who have appropriate data for meta-analyzing). We also discuss how to analyze qualitative data in Chapter 8 and health economics data in Chapter 9.

Step 9: Writing up and editing (Chapters 7, 8, 9 and 10)

This is where you bring all of your hard work together. Step 9 involves writing up your background, methods and results, discussing your findings and drawing conclusions from your review. We discuss how to carry out this step in Chapters 7 and 10, and also touch upon it in Chapter 8 and Chapter 9 for those looking at qualitative evidence and evidence from economic evaluations respectively.

But don't all reviews follow these steps?

When *we* say that we've carried out a *systematic* review of the literature this means that we have clearly planned and fully described the review steps that we've taken; all of our actions are transparent; all of the key methodological decisions have been informed by theory and/or pragmatism and are explicitly set out for the reader to judge. Unfortunately, not all reviews that are published have been written with *our* definition of *systematic* in mind. You may be familiar with the terms 'literature review', 'systematic review', 'narrative review' and 'integrative review' but you might not know exactly what the different terms mean. To complicate matters, in the published literature, these terms are frequently used interchangeably.

Literature reviews

The term 'literature review' is often a common catch-all term for any study that assimilates and synthesizes, or describes, the findings of more than one study.

Narrative reviews

Narrative literature reviews were (historically) and are (currently) typically prepared by 'experts' to provide an overview of a specific topic, to raise over-looked issues and/or identify information gaps, and to encourage new research. Authors of narrative reviews do not usually claim that their reviews are comprehensive. Some of the inherent differences between narrative reviews and systematic reviews, in relation to research process, are displayed in Table 1.2.

Integrative reviews

'Integrative reviews' are a recent development and came into use by researchers as a response to criticism that many systematic reviews only use evidence from RCTs; and that the value of systematic reviews is limited in areas where there is little, or no, trial evidence. To be more inclusive, the term integrative review was coined to reflect a literature review which included both quantitative and qualitative evidence (Sandelowski, Barroso and Voils, 2007). We believe that, with an appropriately stated research question, a single systematic review can include both qualitative and quantitative evidence (and not just evidence from RCTs). However, we believe that students should not be advised to conduct an integrative review as part of their postgraduate study unless they are experienced systematic reviewers. The approach is new and methods for use are evolving.

Table 1.2   Differences in review processes

	Narrative reviews	Systematic reviews
Defining a question	May or may not be clearly defined	Clearly defined and well-focused Always required
Writing a protocol	Not usually required	Recommended/essential
Methodology	Does not follow explicit or rigorous methodology	Follows explicit and rigorous methodology
Searching	No pre-defined search criteria Not necessarily comprehensive Generally relies only on published data Search strategies may be based on expert experience	Exhaustive and with an appropriate balance of sensitivity and specificity Carried out across a number of electronic databases, hand searching of reference lists from relevant papers and high-yield journals and documents/reports Unpublished literature/theses sometimes searched Comprehensive and explicit searching methods used and reported
Definition of inclusion and exclusion criteria	Not essential No selection of studies based on study design	Essential Study design can be selected (for example, only include qualitative data, RCTs or both)
Screening titles and abstracts; selecting full-text papers	Generally carried out by one researcher by reading through relevant papers and based on their own experience	Systematic screening and selection Usually cross-checked by another researcher
Quality assessment	Not necessarily	Yes
Data extraction	Yes	Yes
Analysis and synthesis	No clear method of synthesis	Can involve meta-analysis, narrative or qualitative synthesis
Application	Any field	Any field
Timescale	May be carried out relatively quickly	Can be time consuming due to rigor required
Replication	Not easily replicable	Explicit methods and therefore replicable

A few thoughts before you begin your systematic review

We like to think of the systematic review process as a journey and we use this analogy throughout this book. Experience has taught us that systematic reviewing can be challenging – especially when you don't have a good protocol (map) to guide you. We know that untoward conditions mean that you might have to divert from your chosen route (for example, uncommunicative authors, missing papers, poor quality studies). Experienced systematic reviewers learn to anticipate what is going to happen next. Whether you are travelling on a busy motorway or on a rural lane, it is a good idea to pay attention to your journey time (time management) and plan what to do if your vehicle breaks down (contact your supervisor). Collective experience has taught us how to overcome the most common road hazards and we'd like to share our knowledge with you. In this book, we offer a whole range of tips and strategies to help you begin your journey and reach your final destination.

This chapter has introduced the notion of carrying out a systematic review as part of your Master's thesis. In the majority of the remaining chapters we talk you through the individual steps involved in conducting a systematic review and in Chapter 10 we discuss practical ideas about how you might plan and manage your review. Some of the concepts explored in the book will seem unfamiliar to you at first read, but the advantage of this book is that it hasn't been set out like a novel (that is, written for you to read cover to cover once). We hope that you will start by reading the whole book in chapter order, but we then expect that you will dip in and out of chapters at appropriate points in your research journey. Systematic reviews can be 'bitty' in that you might start a new step before the current one is fully finished. (This might occur, for example, if you are waiting for papers or for input from others.) Each chapter is therefore designed to stand alone.

Frequently Asked Questions

Question 1 Is a systematic review 'real research'?

This is a valid and common question posed by Master's students. There are some researchers and academics who argue that carrying out a systematic review is not 'real research'. We believe that they are wrong. Submitting a systematic review as a research project for a Master's thesis, or as part of a PhD thesis, has become commonplace in many universities and across a variety of different disciplines. We believe that the many learning opportunities that are derived from the systematic review process can help students to achieve academic goals and can equip them with the skills that are required to meet the needs of research communities and enhance their continuing professional development and practices. Indeed, systematic reviews are now regarded as legitimate outputs for the periodic assessments of research conducted within UK universities.

Question 2   Am I taking the easy option with a systematic review?

No, definitely not. Systematic reviewing can be a difficult, time consuming and solitary activity. It's not for the faint-hearted. Whilst you don't (usually) have to go through the ethics process (which can take time and be fraught with difficulties), there are other challenges to face, such as coping with thousands of possible research reports or government documents or, worse yet, finding none. However, the rewards in terms of outputs and learning opportunities make carrying out a systematic review an excellent choice of project for your thesis. For example, it offers an opportunity to display rigorous and reflective practice in your write up and this effort will be acknowledged by the examiner marking your thesis.

Question 3   Can a systematic review form part of a PhD as well as a Master's thesis?

Yes, but it is worth bearing in mind that the focus of the review may differ. Master's students typically need to answer a single specific question, but PhD students tend to use systematic review methodology to describe the literature and/or theory base that informs their primary research. If you are planning to carry out a systematic review to inform a PhD then you may well find yourself conducting a series of mini-systematic reviews rather than one single review that aims to answer a defined and specific question. Alternatively, you might conduct a single systematic review on a very tightly defined topic and go on to conduct a wide-ranging narrative review to situate the results of your systematic review.

Question 4   Can I ask other people to help me with review activities?

If you are planning on publishing your work then collaboration on some specific review activities is essential (for example, searching, cross-checking quality assessment and data extraction). We strongly believe that the best way to conduct a high-quality systematic review is through teamwork, as working independently can be seen as a limitation of the review process. If working independently is your only option, then we believe that you should acknowledge this as a limitation when writing up your thesis.

2

Defining My Review Question and Identifying Inclusion Criteria

M. Gemma Cherry and Rumona Dickson

guide
supervisor studies outcomes
searches methods economics
protocol research systematic
meta-analysis practical quantitative
synthesis student discussion databases management
FAQ post-graduate review
question qualitative searching
quality-assessment data
thesis

This chapter will help you to:

- understand the importance of taking the time to develop, refine and clarify your review question and identify inclusion criteria;
- become aware of the pitfalls and challenges related to the development of a good review question;
- appreciate the value of writing a review protocol;
- be able to deal with challenges, for example, if your review question or methods need to change during the review process.

Introduction

Welcome to the world of systematic reviewing. This chapter is the first of six chapters designed to guide you, step by step, through the systematic review process. We lead you through the process of formulating a clearly structured review question using six practical steps. These steps will help you to focus your systematic review topic. We introduce the role of scoping searches and highlight the importance of discussing your topic with others. The chapter then provides guidance on translating your chosen topic area into a valid and manageable review question. Finally, we include practical advice on how to write your protocol.

Be prepared: good preparation leads to good performance

When embarking upon a research project, two key components are required to ensure a successful and smooth journey: your review question (which tells you your destination) and your review protocol (which details your proposed route and research activities).

The development and refinement of the question is the most important phase of any research project. When carrying out a systematic review, the review question and the review protocol are what you come back to when you are in the middle of the research and feel a bit lost or overwhelmed or confused – which you assuredly will be at one or more points in time. The review question, therefore, needs to be clear, well defined, appropriate, manageable and relevant to the outcomes that you are seeking. Be aware that defining your review question and writing your review protocol may take longer than you think. However, we can assure you that it is a vital investment on your part as it will save you time, energy and distress as your project proceeds.

How do I develop my review question?

We recommend that you follow six steps when developing your review question. These six steps are presented in Table 2.1.

Table 2.1   Developing a review question

Step 1	Identify a topic area of interest to you
Step 2	Carry out early scoping searches
Step 3	Focus your ideas to define the scope of the review
Step 4	Finalize your review question and develop your inclusion criteria
Step 5	Consider contacting experts in the topic area
Step 6	Develop a review protocol

Step 1   Identify a topic area of interest to you

It is important to identify a review question in a topic area that interests you. You will be working on your review for some time and you will need this interest to help you to maintain motivation for the duration of the project. Your topic may be informed by external forces (for example, requirements of your professional practice or your supervisor's research interests); however, the specifics of your research question are likely to be under your control.

Unfortunately, you might have your heart set on addressing a review question only to discover unexpected challenges. For example, someone else may have already published a review addressing your specific question, or there may be very limited research available on your subject of choice, or there may be a massive amount of published research. To manage these challenges we recommend that you keep your topic area broad and remain flexible when initially looking at the available evidence.

Step 2 Carry out early scoping searches

Once you have identified your potential topic area, the next step is to conduct preliminary literature searches, which are frequently called scoping searches and these are discussed more fully in Chapter 3. These do not need to be as comprehensive as the main search that you will use later to identify studies, reports or documents for inclusion in your review. Scoping searches are performed to determine whether your topic area is suitable for a review by giving you a snapshot of the volume and type of evidence available for synthesis. You can choose from a range of electronic databases to search (see Table 3.2 in Chapter 3 which shows many of the most commonly searched databases available). Don't forget to also search PROSPERO, which is an international prospective register of systematic reviews held by the University of York's Centre for Reviews and Dissemination, to check what reviews are currently underway in your topic area. Reading through the results of your scoping searches will quickly let you know if the review that you want to carry out has already been published. If this happens to you then don't panic, just be glad that you have discovered it at this early stage rather than midway through your write up. Look closely at the review that you have found to identify the question that was actually addressed. Is it exactly the same as your question and did the authors use appropriate systematic review methods? When was it published? Has there been research published on the topic since it was published? If so, then there may be a rationale for updating the existing published review. If not and/or you see too much overlap then you will need to reformulate or adapt your review question. Think of it like planning an alternative route because of a road closure – it's a nuisance but far better to re-route before you set off.

Scoping searches also allow you to identify the individuals or groups of researchers who are leaders in your topic area of interest. They may also highlight a variety of (perhaps disparate) viewpoints. Published research studies frequently contain a section that outlines future research directions; it can be useful to read these to see if your proposed review question is mentioned or if authors have called for a synthesis of available evidence before more empirical research is conducted. If this is the case then it is a good sign that there is a gap in the research evidence that your review could fill.

The results of scoping searches tell you how much published literature and information are available in your topic area. For example, from the results of your scoping searches you will know if there is little or no published research in your topic area, a common fear raised by many of the students we supervise. When we are asked, 'How little is too little?' the answer that we give is that this depends on the purpose of your review. For example, if the purpose of your review is to demonstrate to your examiners that you are able to identify, synthesize and critically appraise literature, then including zero papers in your review will be inappropriate. You might then think about expanding your review question to include wider groups of participants, more interventions or different outcomes (see Frequently Asked Questions at the end of this chapter). However, if you are carrying out a review to inform your own professional practice, then you may want to continue with your original question, particularly if you are thinking of applying for a grant to fund primary research. Many funders make it a requirement that a systematic review is carried out prior to funding approval to show that there is a need for the research. If there is no published evidence it is generally appropriate to use the (rather thin) review to demonstrate that your research has identified a gap in knowledge.

On the other hand, some students find that their scoping searches end up returning hundreds of published papers or documents. We are often asked, 'How much is too much?' If this happens you might want to think about narrowing your review question. For example, perhaps choose a more specific population, comparator, intervention, outcome or setting. Look at some of the published papers in the topic area to get a sense of how to narrow your review question. For example, if your interest is in adolescent pregnancy, you may want to consider the lived experiences of pregnant adolescents. Is there a certain stage of pregnancy in which you are interested? Are you only interested in pregnant adolescents in a specific country? Considering different perspectives will help you to focus your question and will yield a more manageable and homogenous set of evidence.

Do not be disheartened if, at this stage, you have to modify, expand or reject a topic area or review question because your scoping searches identify an evidence base that is different to the one that you expected (or hoped) to find – this is very common. The aim of scoping searches is to formulate an idea of the current state of knowledge relating to your topic. It is like studying a map before starting a journey so that you get the lay of the land and are able to explore different travel options.

Step 3   Focus your ideas to define the scope of the review

Once you have identified a topic area and conducted early scoping searches to determine the volume and type of literature available and the important current issues, the next stage is to focus on the direction that you want your review to take. It is at this stage that it is important to produce a short summary of your ideas (no more than one side of A4 paper) and explore these ideas with your supervisor and/or peers to solicit their views. If possible, it may also be worthwhile attending a live or online conference in the topic area to get a sense of the current research issues relating to your chosen topic. A mind map of the results of your earlier scoping searches can be a useful means of summarizing your ideas and may highlight key issues that you had not previously considered. Figure 2.1 provides an example of the way in which a topic area can be refined into a number of possible review questions.

The example shown in Figure 2.1 is typical of the refinement of a research question relating to fever in children. You can see that there are a number of different ways to approach such a broad topic area of interest and a number of potential review questions. For example, you could consider current guidelines for treating fever in children and systematically

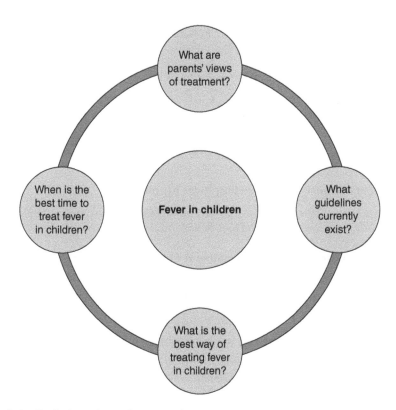

Figure 2.1   Evolution of a review question

review them; you could take a qualitative approach and systematically review research reporting parents' views on treating fever in children; or you could consider the best method or time to treat fever (for example, when first presented or after 12 hours). Each review question requires its own specific methods of searching for evidence and synthesizing data so it's important to consider all of the options before finalizing your review question (see Box 2.1 for more detail).

Box 2.1

Evolution from general idea to final review question

Qualitative or quantitative evidence?

Students often ask, 'Should my systematic review include qualitative or quantitative evidence, or both?' The answer to this lies with your review question and choosing the evidence that best helps you to answer that question. Consider again the fever in children example. Figure 2.1 displayed a number of possible ways that you could choose to systematically review the research in this area.

a) When is the best time to treat fever in children?

This approach lends itself best to quantitative evidence. The variable of interest is a quantifiable concept (time) and therefore the outcome that you are interested in would be efficacy of treatment at a certain time point after the initial onset of fever. Doctors' or parents' views on the best time to treat fever would not be very useful in this case.

b) What is the best way of treating fever in children?

This too is a quantitative question. You may be interested in the clinical effectiveness of a new drug for lowering fever. Does it work quickly? Does it have side effects?

c) What are parents' views on treatment of fever in children?

In this case you are interested in considering parents' views on the best way to treat fever in children and qualitative research findings would provide a rich source of data.

d) What guidelines for treating fever in children currently exist?

This question can only be answered by quantitative evidence and would be addressed through a review of existing guidelines for, perhaps, health care workers or parents.

By this stage, you may have spent a lot of time and invested a great deal of energy in your chosen topic area and the thought of starting again or changing your approach might not be welcome. However, it is important to consult and consider the views of others, especially experts in the field. It is far better for your topic area to change or evolve at this stage rather than after the review is under way. It might require a little more reading or literature searching, but consideration of the opinions and ideas raised in your discussions with supervisors and/or professional colleagues is time well spent.

Step 4   Finalize your review question and develop your inclusion criteria

Now it is time to finalize your review question. Up until now you have approached your systematic review as a topic area that interests you. It is at this point that this abstract concept begins to take shape as a review question.

Your review question is a formal statement of the intention of your systematic review. It is a statement that develops from what you know (as identified through examination of available evidence) to what it is that you want to know, or know more, about. A review question is different from a hypothesis because a hypothesis states the probable direction of a relationship between variables, whereas a systematic review question always ends with a question mark and is always connected to a body of existing knowledge. A systematic review question can be descriptive (presenting a concept), normative (questions that explore preferences about what should happen), observational or relational (investigating a relationship between two or more variables), causal (investigating the effect of one or more independent variables on one or more outcome variables) or theoretical (exploring factors that cause a condition, event or process). Examples of review questions relating to infection control in hospitals are displayed in Table 2.2.

A good systematic review question should be motivating and spark your own thoughts and interests, be researchable (that is, can be completed to a high standard within the timelines set and resources available), be neither too broad nor too narrow and have a focus on information that is available (that is, published literature) and accessible (that is, available to you).

There is always a dilemma about how broad a review question should be. It is our experience that most students try to answer questions that are too broad and they end up looking at too much evidence. This may result

Table 2.2   Different types of review question

Type	Example review question
Descriptive	What are the trends in hospital-acquired infections over the last ten years in the UK?
Normative	How do health care professionals perceive the care delivery issues relating to allocation of scarce infection control resources in rural hospitals?
Observational/relational	Is there a relationship between hospital-acquired infections and death rates in hospitals?
Causal	Do structured educational interventions have an impact on the number of hospital-acquired infections?
Theoretical	What reasons do health care professionals give for non-compliance with infection-control policies in hospitals?

in an unmanageable body of literature to synthesize later in the review process. To avoid your question ending up too broad, think about narrowing the 'who, what, how and where' of your research question; this is a good place to start when developing inclusion criteria for use in your review.

Inclusion criteria

Inclusion criteria describe the specific attributes that a study must have if it is to be included in your review; they are sometimes known as eligibility criteria. Development of your inclusion criteria and review question often occur in parallel; to some extent your review question will define your inclusion criteria, but thinking specifically about inclusion criteria can also help you to narrow and focus your review question. For example, consideration of inclusion criteria allows you to identify where your review question may be ambiguous or too specific – the two tasks should be seen as complementary rather than separate.

Table 2.3 gives an example showing refinement of a review question and how this feeds into the development of inclusion criteria regardless of whether the evidence considered as part of the review is qualitative, quantitative or both. It is common to include study design as an inclusion criterion – this is not addressed by 'who, what, how and where' questions. Remember, the questions set out in Table 2.3 can be supplemented with other criteria.

Another way to develop inclusion criteria, used predominantly in systematic reviews of effectiveness, is to generate a PICO table (a further

Table 2.3   Example of a 'who, what, how and where' table

	Points for consideration			
Review question	**Who**	**What**	**How**	**Where**
What influences communication in health care?	**Not specified.** Needs further definition. Will participants be doctors? Nurses? Patients? A mixture?	**Not specified.** Needs further definition. What will be reviewed in relation to communication in health care? Associations with variables? Individuals' narratives relating to communication?	**Communication.** Needs further definition. With other health care professionals? With patients? With relatives? Written communication? Verbal or non-verbal communication? How will it be measured?	**Not specified.** Needs further definition. Acute care? Primary care? All health care settings?
How do individual characteristics of health care professionals influence communication?	**Health care professionals.** Still needs further definition – see above.	**Individual characteristics.** More information provided than above but the term 'individual characteristics' is still unclear. Whose individual characteristics? Needs further clarification.	**Communication.** Still needs further definition – see above.	**Not specified.** Still needs further definition – see above.
How does the personality of mental health nurses influence their ability to communicate with their patients as measured using standardized scales in routine practice?	**Mental health nurses.**	**Personality (measured using standardized scales).** What is the definition of a standardized scale? Needs further clarification.	**Communication with their patients.** How is this assessed? Using self-report questionnaires for patients? Professional opinions? Qualitative or quantitative research considered? Needs further clarification.	**Routine practice setting.** This is clear and defined.

development of the 'who, what, how and where' table). PICO stands for population, intervention, comparator and outcome. Occasionally people also include Setting and Study Design. An example of a PICO table assessing the evidence for reading as an intervention is shown in Table 2.4.

Table 2.4   A detailed and comprehensive PICO table

Review question	What is the evidence for reading aloud and group reading as therapeutic interventions to improve the health and well-being of patients with neurological disorders in clinical and long-term care settings?
Population	Adults and children with any neurological disease or insult, progressive or traumatic.
Intervention	Individual reading; reading aloud; reading in groups.
	Any form of reading used either as a therapeutic intervention or as an activity to identify therapeutic benefit and/or improve health or well-being.
Comparator	The stated interventions compared with each other, placebo or no intervention.
Outcomes	Any positive or adverse health-based outcome, any objective health-based clinical outcome measure. Any subjective outcome whether identified through thematic analysis or quantitative data collection methods.
Setting	Hospital wards, rehabilitation centers, nursing and residential homes, respite centers and hospices. Outpatient and community settings.
Study design	All.

The PICO table shown in Table 2.4 is detailed and clearly defines the key components of the research question. Whether you are carrying out a quantitative or qualitative review, it is essential to go through the process of clearly defining your review question. If, after this stage, you feel confident that your review question has not previously been considered, that it is unique and that it reflects appropriate characteristics of the topic area, then it is time to move on to the next stage. The important point to remember is not to get disheartened if you need to carry out further work on your review question at this stage.

Step 5   Consider contacting experts in the topic area

At this point you should have a well-developed and well-defined review question (and inclusion criteria) and be able to populate your 'who, what, how and where' table or your PICO table. You may decide that you want to contact experts in your topic area. As a rule of thumb we suggest that if the purpose of your review is to learn more about specific aspects of published research then you should carry out some background reading to familiarize yourself with the views of key opinion holders. If feasible, consider logging into an online conference or presentation to get a sense of expert thinking and, most importantly, what the leaders in the field consider to be the gaps in the literature. On the other hand, if you are conducting the review to inform your professional practice then it may be more critical to directly contact experts in the field. The purpose of the contact would be to ensure that you are indeed on the right track in relation to currently accepted practice. If you choose to contact experts then we suggest you should be well versed in your topic area before you approach them and be very clear about what it is you want from them. As you would expect, a generic email saying you are a Master's student doing a review and want their help is unlikely to receive a response. However, a well thought out email (as shown in Box 2.2), explaining your review question, its importance to your professional practice and a set of well-defined questions, has a good chance of receiving a response.

Box 2.2

Example of a well thought out email

Dear Professor Smith

Re: Systematic review of non-pharmacological treatments for the management of agitation in patients with psychotic illness

I would be very grateful if you could advise me on an aspect of the review that I am currently conducting as part of my Master's studies at the University of Liverpool. The preliminary aim of the review is to examine the efficacy of non-pharmacological treatments for the management of agitation in patients with psychotic illness. I've completed my scoping searches and have identified several relevant systematic reviews in the area (please see attached). As a published expert in this clinical area, please could you have a quick read through this list and let me know if you are aware of any pertinent systematic reviews that I may have missed during my searches and/ or if you know of any ongoing reviews that are due to be published in the next 3 months? This will help me to ensure that I am addressing a novel question which has not previously been addressed.

Thank you very much for your help.

Yours sincerely

Student

Step 6   Develop a review protocol

Good news – you are almost ready to begin your review! You have a research question (the destination); now you need to write a review protocol (which explains how you will get there). This is a very important stage and should not be skipped. Every piece of quality research is guided by a research protocol. No researcher would consider conducting a randomized controlled trial (RCT) without a protocol, and your systematic review is just as important a piece of research and deserves to have an overall plan. It will also help you as the review progresses as it acts as a guide to steer your decision making.

A well thought out protocol describes the current evidence base, identifies the question that the review will address and outlines the methods that will be used to answer the question. Table 2.5 provides a guide to the sections

Table 2.5   Example of a protocol structure

Title	Content
Background	The background section can be developed from the results of your scoping search. This section should be a brief summary of your 'who, what, how and where' table and also provide a context for the review. This text can eventually form the background section of your thesis.
Summary of existing literature	This summary will provide an overview of the literature that is important to the review question. This section should end with a rationale explaining why the review question is important and why it needs to be addressed.
Research question and aims	Present the research question and any research aims in as much detail as possible.
Methods 　**Search strategy** 　**Screening and selecting** 　**Quality assessment** 　**Data extraction** 　**Data analysis**	This is the section where you lay out the road map which details what you will do during the review process and how long you think each task will take. Under the heading of search strategy, we recommend that you describe the resources that you want to search and give summary details of how you will look for published literature (for example, journal articles and conference proceedings) and, if appropriate, unpublished literature (for example, registry data and government reports). In a protocol, you don't have to list all the specific search terms you used; however, it is good practice to provide one example search strategy in an Appendix. It should then go on to describe how data will be quality assessed, what data will be extracted, who will do each task and how the data will be analyzed. If planning to carry out a meta-analysis then you need to think about subgroups and heterogeneity in advance.
Time frame	A plan of how long you anticipate that each important review activity might take.

you may want to consider including in your review protocol. These sections do not need to be followed exactly but writing a clear protocol based on them will help you set out your work plan and will also serve as a guide that you can return to during the research process. Most of the chapters in this book end with a list of 'Key points to consider when writing your protocol'. Furthermore, we include a list of 'What an examiner is looking for in your thesis' at the end of each chapter. Don't forget to make use of these handy guides when writing your protocol.

Begin your review

You are now ready to start your review. If you've taken our advice, your review question will be well focused and you will have clearly stated inclusion criteria and a clearly written protocol. Your next step is to search for relevant evidence. It's now time for you to put what you've learnt into practice.

Key points to consider when writing your protocol

- Results of scoping searches can help you to describe the quality and quantity of relevant evidence available;
- It is important to make a case for why your review question is important and needs to be addressed;
- Clearly stated inclusion and exclusion criteria are essential to the successful completion of your review.

What an examiner is looking for in your thesis

- Evidence of scoping searches;
- A well set-out systematic review question – this lets the examiner know you have carefully considered the different components of the question;
- An explicit statement of your inclusion criteria.

Frequently Asked Questions

Question 1   How long will it take to develop my review question and
produce my protocol?

This is a valid and common question asked by Master's students and unfortunately the answer is 'How long is a piece of string?' It will depend on the
topic area, your experience in the topic area, the amount of published
research available, the clarity of the original idea, the length of time it takes
to hear back from your supervisor(s) and others involved in your review, the
amount of time you can dedicate to it (that is, full-time or part-time) and
many other variables. This is the stage of your review where you will consider different options and this will take time, but remember 'failing to
prepare means preparing to fail'. Whatever time is spent on this stage will
be time saved later because you will have a clear question and plan that will
guide your review.

Question 2   What if I can't define my inclusion criteria?

It is our experience that students often fail to clearly define aspects of their
inclusion criteria. For example, the population might be very broad – such
as adults with diabetes. It might be necessary to define the population more
specifically as 'adults with newly diagnosed diabetes' – which would identify a population totally different from people diagnosed with diabetes in
childhood. If you are finding it difficult to define your inclusion criteria at
an early stage then you will most definitely struggle when it comes to putting searches together or deciding which papers are relevant. Clearly
defined inclusion criteria will save you time and reduce stress later in the
review process.

Question 3   What if I lose interest in the topic half-way through the
review?

Unfortunately, this is something that sometimes happens to students and
often can't be helped, particularly as you will be investing a lot of time and
energy in the review. This is why we strongly encourage you to pick a topic
area that interests you. For example, we often suggest that students carry out

reviews in areas that are of interest to the health and/or welfare of a family member, or that will be used as part of their professional practice. However, as this is a relatively short-term research project we hope that you will stay motivated throughout the research process. It is worth knowing that all researchers, at some point in a research project, will wonder why they ever began the project.

Question 4   Do I have to write a review protocol?

Simply put, it is good practice to write, and then refer to, a review protocol. Having a protocol will make your research journey easier and will help you to plan research activities, guide your decision making and show what progress you have made.

3

Developing My Search Strategy and Applying Inclusion Criteria

Yenal Dundar and Nigel Fleeman

guide
supervisor studies outcomes
searches methods economics
protocol research systematic
practical
meta-analysis quantitative
synthesis student discussion databases management
FAQ post-graduate review
question qualitative searching
quality-assessment data
thesis

This chapter will help you to:

- understand the difference between scoping searches and a main search;
- formulate a search strategy;
- judge the most appropriate bibliographic resources that you need to search;
- screen the titles and abstracts of potentially eligible studies and select full-text papers for inclusion;
- report the methods and results of your search for evidence.

Introduction

This chapter guides you through the processes of searching for, screening and selecting studies for inclusion in your review. We provide guidance on what is involved in searching for evidence, where and how to store the results of your searches, and how the results should be screened using inclusion criteria to determine whether individual papers should be included in your systematic review.

What is meant by searching and what does it entail?

Searching is a term that is used to describe the methods by which you identify evidence to be included in your review. Potential resources include bibliographic databases, volumes of specialist journals, reference lists from retrieved articles, research registers, government databases, newspapers and/or experts in your particular field.

Before you begin your main search it is worth taking some time to think through exactly how comprehensive your search needs to be. In a gold standard review that aims to inform policy or practice, your goal would be to identify *all* of the available evidence relevant to your review question. Some argue that it is essential that you find *all* of the evidence that is out there, no matter how long it takes. The counter-argument is that it is not worth spending long periods of time conducting searches that only find one additional obscure study with information that will not, in all probability, change the overall results of the review. As a student it is possible, but unlikely, that your systematic review will be used to inform policy but it may be used to help you change your professional practice. Therefore, we recommend a pragmatic approach to searching; this means that searches should be carried out using logical and systematic methods in an attempt to identify the available evidence needed to address your review question. You just need to make sure that your search is balanced in terms of specificity (it identifies the relevant papers) and sensitivity (it does not identify too many irrelevant papers). It is possible that, in the time you have available, you may not be able to be exhaustive in your searching. What you do need to do is address the fact that your review may not include all available information if this is, in fact, the case. You will need to discuss how this might affect the conclusions that you draw and the recommendations that you make (discussed further in Chapter 7).

The second thing to think about before you begin searching for evidence to help you answer your review question is where you will search. You would be wasting your time searching for articles on social work policy in an economics only database. Similarly, if you are looking for evidence of public opinion relating to a recent government policy decision you would not look in a database of medical journals, but would look in newspaper archives. You need to make sure that you are sufficiently familiar with the data sources available to you so that you can plan to search those that are most appropriate.

The third thing to remember is that, no matter what you are doing, it is always good to have help. When it comes to searching for studies, a helping hand can come from an information specialist or librarian who is familiar with searching electronic databases. These specialists are just that – they have specialist knowledge of the information that is kept and indexed electronically and have a good idea of how to interrogate specialist databases efficiently. When you take your research question to specialists you may be surprised (pleasantly, we hope) that they approach your research question from different perspectives and can help you to explore your question more fully. We are often amazed at the different perspectives brought by colleagues who see things through a different kaleidoscope.

Scoping searches

Scoping searches differ from the main search that you perform in your systematic review. Scoping searches (as discussed in Chapter 2) are designed to provide an overview of the literature to help you to locate a sufficient number of key references quickly (for example, studies and other reviews published on your research topic) to allow you to gain a clearer understanding of the key issues in your topic area and subsequently to develop your review question. When carrying out scoping searches you don't need to search all of the available resources – a couple of data sources will likely be sufficient. Using simple search terms, the results will give you an idea of how many studies you are likely to find when you carry out your main search. They can thus be used as a starting point for the development of a search strategy. Scoping searches are important as they help you to determine the subsequent direction of your review. They need to be carried out at the start of your project, prior to finalizing your research question and writing your review protocol. You may, or may not, need to report the details of your scoping searches in your thesis. Ask your supervisor if there is a departmental preference or, to be on the safe side, include details in an Appendix.

What is a search strategy and how do I formulate one?

Once you have carried out your scoping searches, focused your research question and written your protocol, the next step is to develop your search strategy. This strategy is a description of the methods you will use to identify evidence and explains in detail how you will search for relevant published and/or unpublished evidence specific to your review question. Table 3.1 summarizes the steps involved when formulating a search strategy.

It is worth noting that the term 'search strategy' means different things to different people. To some, it covers the specific terms that are used when searching a single database (for example, key search terms or specific years to be searched). To others, it describes the global approach to searching

Table 3.1   Key steps to consider when formulating a search strategy

Step 1	Consider the different types of information available to you
Step 2	Identify the specific resources that you will search
Step 3	Identify the key search terms that you will use
Step 4	Outline your plans for minimizing bias
Step 5	Plan how you are going to store and save the results of your search

(sometimes called the 'search plan') and covers all the activities involved in the main searches (for example, specific databases or other resources to be searched, key search terms and any date limits).

Box 3.1 presents a detailed search strategy from one of our recent systematic review reports (Fleeman et al., 2011). This example shows the resources, key search terms and time periods that were used in the main searches. If you look closely you will see the very subtle differences in key search terms that were used to find relevant publications in two different databases. When searching several resources, information specialists can advise you on how to tweak your key search terms to ensure that your searches are capable of identifying the data that you need. This is one of the reasons that we recommend that you work with information specialists – they are familiar with the unique features of different databases and can help you to use appropriate search terms. They will also remind you to use both technical terms (for example, neoplasm) and lay terms (for example, cancer). Finally, don't forget that there are often UK spellings (for example, tumour) and US spellings (for example, tumor) of the same word.

Box 3.1

Example of a search strategy

The following databases were searched with the following search terms. All databases were searched on 9 May 2010.

Ovid MEDLINE 1980 to April week 4 2010

1 (lapatinib OR tykerb OR tyverb OR lapatinib ditosylate).af.
2 (trastuzumab OR herceptin).af.
3 (letrozole OR femara OR anastrozole OR arimidex OR exemestane OR aromasin).af.
4 exp Aromatase Inhibitors/
5 aromatase inhibitor$.tw.
6 1 OR 2
7 3 OR 5
8 6 AND 7
9 exp Breast Neoplasms/
10 (breast$adj5 (neoplasm$ OR cancer$ OR tumo?r$ OR carcinoma$ OR adenocarcinoma$ OR sarcoma$ OR dcis OR ductal OR infiltrat$ OR intraductal$ OR lobular OR medullary)).mp.

```
11  9 OR 10
12  8 AND 11
```

EMBASE 1980 to week 18 2010

```
1   (lapatinib OR tykerb OR tyverb OR lapatinib ditosylate).af.
2   (trastuzumab OR herceptin).af.
3   (letrozole OR femara OR anastrozole OR arimidex OR exemestane OR aro-
    masin).af.
4   Aromatase Inhibitors.mp. OR exp aromatase inhibitor/
5   1 OR 2
6   3 OR 4
7   5 AND 6
8   (breast$adj5 (neoplasm$ OR cancer$ OR tumo?r$ OR carcinoma$ OR
    adenocarcinoma$ OR sarcoma$ OR dcis OR ductal OR infiltrat$ OR
    intraductal$ OR lobular OR medullary)).mp.
9   exp breast cancer/
10  8 OR 9
11  7 AND 10
```

Step 1 Consider the different types of information available to you

Evidence can be published or unpublished; the latter is known as gray or
fugitive literature. The main sources of published evidence include bibliographic databases, volumes of specialist journals, reference lists from
already retrieved articles and/or newspaper archives. The main sources of
unpublished evidence include research registers, academic databases and
government databases. Databases and research registers are searched electronically, while reference lists frequently require manual searches – often
called hand searching.

Searching bibliographic databases

The most commonly searched sources of evidence are bibliographic databases which are available electronically on CD-ROM or via the Internet. The
structure in which they are accessed is commonly referred to as a Platform
or Interface. Bibliographic databases contain records of articles from a number of journals and sometimes books, book chapters, newspapers, theses
and/or conference abstracts. These records will, as a minimum, include a
title, author(s) and a source (for example, journal article). Most databases

relate to a particular discipline, although some are multi-disciplinary in content which is why it is important to know what it is you are looking for so you can select the most appropriate databases. While some databases can be accessed without charge by the general public via the Internet, the majority are available on a subscription only basis. If your institution does not have a subscription to a database that you want to search, speak to your institution's librarian who might be able to get you temporary access.

Hand searching

The concept of hand searching has evolved over time. In the early days of conducting systematic reviews (up to around the 1990s) researchers did not have access to extensive electronic databases that listed both past, current and upcoming publications. It was therefore necessary to go to the library and literally hand search the journals of interest to identify relevant papers (and then make photocopies of potentially eligible papers). While literal hand searches may still be undertaken, increasingly hand searching more commonly entails searches of electronic tables of contents of key journals to identify potential articles of interest. Literal hand searches might be of particular value if your review takes a historical perspective and you need to examine specific documents held in specialist libraries or document storage areas. Having said this, resources that are available electronically change almost daily. For example, the British Library (British Library Archives, 2013) and the Library of Congress (Library of Congress, 2013) now have excellent online archives of British and US newspapers. So when you refer to hand searching in your thesis, you probably mean manually searching electronic tables of contents or journals rather than literal hand searching!

Step 2   Identify the specific resources you want to search

The specific resources that you decide to search will depend on your particular discipline and/or research question. Examples of some common databases are presented (by discipline) in Table 3.2. This table by no means contains an exhaustive list but rather is intended as a guide.

The number of specific resources that you need to search depends on the purpose of your review. If the aim of your research is to derive a theory to

Table 3.2 Databases and other sources of information by discipline

Database	Platform/Interface
Multi-disciplinary	
Copac*	http://copac.ac.uk/
Google Scholar*	scholar.google.com/
JSTOR	www.jstor.org/
ProQuest Dissertations & Theses (PQDT)	ProQuest
SCOPUS	SciVerse
Web of Knowledge	Thomson Reuters
Zetoc*	http://zetoc.mimas.ac.uk
Criminal Justice	
The Home Office (UK Government)*	www.homeoffice.gov.uk/
National Criminal Justice	EBSCO Host
The US NCJRS (National Criminal Justice Reference Service) Abstracts Database*	www.ncjrs.gov/App/AbstractDB/AbstractDBSearch.aspx
Economics	
EconLit	EBSCO Host
HEED (Health Economic Evaluation Database)	Wiley Online Library
Education	
EPPI Centre (The Evidence for Policy and Practice Information and Co-ordinating Centre)*	http://eppi.ioe.ac.uk/cms/
ERIC	EBSCO Host
Educational Research Abstracts Online	Ingenta
Health	
CINAHL	EBSCO Host
Cochrane Library* (including DARE, HTA, NHS EED)	http://onlinelibrary.wiley.com/o/cochrane/cochrane_clcentral_articles_fs.html
EMBASE	Ovid
HTA database*	www.crd.york.ac.uk/CRDWeb/SearchPage.asp
MEDLINE	Ovid, EBSCO Host
PROSPERO	www.crd.york.ac.uk/NIHR_PROSPERO
PubMed*	www.ncbi.nlm.nih.gov/pubmedhealth/

(Continued)

Table 3.2   (Continued)

Database	Platform/Interface
History and Humanities	
America: History & Life	EBSCO Host
British Humanities Index	ProQuest
British Periodicals	ProQuest
ProQuest Historical Newspapers	ProQuest
Social Sciences	
ASSIA (Applied Social Sciences Index and Abstracts)	ProQuest
Campbell Collaboration Library of Systematic Reviews	www.campbellcollaboration.org/library.php
CORDIS*	http://cordis.europa.eu/newsearch/index.cfm?page=advSearch
PsycINFO	www.apa.org/pubs/databases/psycinfo/index.aspx
Sociological Abstracts	ProQuest
Social Sciences Index	Thomson Reuters

* Free to access without the need for subscription

explain a particular phenomenon, then you will need to consider the different research approaches that exist to derive theories (for example, grounded theory or deviant case analysis), and you will require a wide range, as opposed to an exhaustive amount, of evidence. As such, a broad search across a large number of resources is likely to be required. However, if the aim of your research is to examine the clinical effectiveness of a particular medical intervention, then your search would likely be focused on specific medical databases.

Step 3   Identify the key search terms you will use

No doubt you are familiar with searching the Internet via search engines such as Google or Google Scholar, where you type a number of search terms relevant to whatever it is you are trying to find. However, you will probably be less familiar with searching specialist bibliographic databases. The majority of bibliographic databases enable you to be more precise and use more advanced and complex searches than those that you would use when searching the Internet. This is because most bibliographic databases have more than just one box (i.e., field) in which to add text terms. You can also combine

Table 3.3   Use of Boolean operators when searching for evidence

Boolean operator	Function	Examples
AND	Narrows the search and identifies references containing **all** of the words entered	(education AND university) This search retrieves records containing both the words 'education' and 'university'
OR	Broadens the search and identifies references containing **any** of the words entered	(education OR university) This search retrieves records containing either the word 'education' or the word 'university'
NOT	Narrows search and identifies references that **do not** contain the term following it	(education NOT university) This search retrieves records containing the word 'education' but excludes those which also contain the word 'university'

the terms entered in each box by using 'AND', 'OR' and 'NOT', also known as Boolean operators (see Table 3.3).

Searching specific fields also allows you to limit your searches and specify search parameters, for example, by year or language. In addition, most bibliographic databases offer you the option of using 'wildcards' (commonly a question mark (?), an asterisk (*) or a symbol such as '$'). These enable you to search for part of a word (for example, 'wom?n' will find 'woman' and 'women'; 'psychiatr*' will find 'psychiatrist', 'psychiatry' or 'psychiatric'), to search for a whole word which may have different spellings (for example, 'behavi*r' will find 'behavior' and 'behaviour'), or to include a search term and its plural (for example, 'trial$' will identify 'trial' and 'trials').

Free-text words are words located anywhere in the title, abstract or main text of the article. Subject headings or index terms are used to index the content of bibliographic databases. All databases have their own list of particular subject headings. For example, Medical Subject Headings (MeSH) are a list of subject headings used for indexing articles for MEDLINE and PubMed. When conducting a MEDLINE search via PubMed, search terms are automatically mapped to the corresponding MeSH terms, making the searching of databases easier. You can refer to the US National Library of Medicine for further information on MeSH terms (US National Library of Medicine, 2013).

Using a combination of free-text words (for example, breast cancer OR breast tumor OR breast neoplasm OR breast carcinoma) and appropriate subject headings (for example, 'Breast Neoplasms') in your search strategy is considered good practice and should improve the accuracy of your search results.

Keywords are words assigned to publications to highlight the important topics or subjects being discussed (for example, randomized controlled trial (RCT), a specific type of exposure or particular group of participants) and they appear in a separate field in the database. When deciding on your search terms, it is often helpful to identify the database record for a study that you have already identified as being important, see what keywords were used to index it and then use the same words to begin your main search. Repeating this process, using a number of pre-identified references, can help you to build up the key terms for your search.

Finally, it is important to realize that producing an optimal search strategy for a specific bibliographic database can take time and is likely to be an iterative process. It is highly unlikely that your first attempt will result in identifying the optimal search terms to use (and if you think it has, it will be worth double checking). Remember, one size does not fit all when it comes to searching and you need to develop different searches for different databases; your information specialist should be able to help you finalize your searches. For your thesis, you will need to keep accurate records of how many citations you obtain via each search. Remember to check that the key studies you identified from your scoping searches are identified by your main search – if not, you need to go back and revise your search strategy until these studies are identified. It is also a good idea to copy and paste your search strategy and make a note of your results so that you know exactly how your search was configured.

Step 4 Outline your plans for minimizing bias

There are a number of issues relating to bias that need to be considered when planning your searches. First, you need to think about publication bias. It is well known that studies which report positive findings are most likely to be submitted by authors for publication; these types of studies are also more likely to be selected for publication than studies which report negative findings. Therefore, you need to consider whether the published studies identified by your search are representative of all of the studies conducted.

Second, you might like to consider location bias as studies are sometimes published in journals which are not indexed in bibliographic databases and therefore may not be identified by your electronic search (for example, government reports). This means that there is value in searching the gray literature, such as abstracts of conferences to identify studies that have been recently conducted but have not (yet) been published and/or that are ongoing. It should be noted that the gray literature may not be peer reviewed in the same way that a study published in an academic journal is likely to be, which in itself may add further bias. In an attempt to identify all of the studies that address your review question, you might want to search registries of studies. For example, if you are searching for RCTs, you can check the ClinicalTrials.gov website (US National Institutes of Health, 2013). Since September 2007, by law, all RCTs in the US must be registered at ClinicalTrials.gov and other countries also strongly encourage the registration of clinical trials. Registries for other types of studies also exist (for example, the UK Economic and Social Research Council's research catalogue (Economic and Social Research Council, 2013)).

Third, you need to think about language bias. This occurs because studies which report positive findings are most likely to be published in English-language journals and studies with negative findings are more likely to be published in local-language journals. So you need to consider the implications of restricting your search to English-language only papers.

Finally, if you are searching for evidence that is only reported in full-text format, you may miss out on the most up-to-date evidence; an example of this would be the results of studies that have recently been reported at a conference, as these studies may be available in abstract format only. If you do include abstract only evidence, then you need to acknowledge the limitations of this type of evidence in your report (for example, limited information available and the fact that early results do not always match final results).

Step 5 Plan where you are going to save and store the results of your search

The use of bibliographic software such as EndNote or Ref Works is encouraged during the review process, especially if you have a lot of included studies. Such software packages not only allow for direct exportation of citations (and their abstracts) from the Internet and bibliographic databases, but they also have tools that enable you to easily identify (and then delete) duplicate records. Bibliographic software packages are also extremely useful when extracting data, synthesizing results and writing up your thesis. For example, these packages allow you to sort references into relevant groups, such as all included studies, all studies with the same endpoint and references relating to different sections of your thesis. Furthermore, the software enables you to directly insert references into your thesis and in the referencing style (for example, Harvard or Vancouver) required by your academic institution. Chapter 10 discusses bibliographic software further.

Choosing your included studies

Once you have finalized and conducted your main search, you are ready to press ahead and screen and select studies for inclusion in your review. Table 3.4 outlines the key steps involved when choosing your included studies.

Table 3.4   Key steps to consider when choosing your included studies

Step 1	De-duplicate references and pilot use of inclusion criteria
Step 2	Screen all titles and abstracts identified via searches using inclusion criteria (Stage 1)
Step 3	Obtain full-text papers of all potentially eligible articles
Step 4	Apply inclusion criteria and select full-text papers for inclusion in review (Stage 2)
Step 5	Report results of your searches (using PRISMA diagram)

Step 1   De-duplicate references and pilot use of inclusion criteria

Before you apply your criteria to your long list of potentially relevant studies, you need to de-duplicate your references and pilot your screening and selection tools. This is simply the identification and deletion of any duplicate references that have shown up in your main search results. Duplicates are almost inevitable if you have searched more than one resource. If you have stored your references using bibliographic software it should be possible to merge search results from different databases and then easily remove any duplicates automatically. However, only minor differences in how a reference is indexed in different databases will mean that some duplicates will be missed and so you should aim to remove these manually. It is important to stress that duplicates are the only references you should ever delete. You should always know how many references your search has identified and how many references were duplicates.

After removing any duplicates, it is a good idea to pilot the application of your inclusion criteria. You need to incorporate your inclusion criteria within a tool that you can use to screen titles and abstracts and then use to select full-text papers for inclusion in the review. You can use a paper version or an electronic version of your form to apply inclusion criteria; it is your choice. An example of a screening/selection tool is shown in Table 3.5. For Stage 1

Table 3.5 Review question + inclusion criteria = screening/selection tool

Review question: What is the clinical effectiveness of first-line chemotherapy in addition to radiotherapy for adult patients with locally advanced non-small cell lung cancer?

Inclusion criteria (based on PICOS):
Population = adult patients with non-small cell lung cancer;
Intervention = chemotherapy + radiotherapy;
Comparator = chemotherapy + radiotherapy;
Outcomes = overall survival;
Study design = RCT.

CHEMOTHERAPY + RADIOTHERAPY SCREENING AND SELECTION TOOL		
Reviewer name:		**Date:**
Author name/Study ID:		**Year:**
Title:		**Journal:**
Patient population	Include	Exclude
	☐ Adults with non-small cell lung cancer	☐ Adults with other cancers ☐ Children
Interventions	Include	Exclude
	☐ Chemotherapy + radiotherapy	☐ Chemotherapy only ☐ Radiotherapy only
Comparators	Include	Exclude
	☐ Chemotherapy + radiotherapy	☐ Chemotherapy only ☐ Radiotherapy only
Outcomes	**Must include**	Exclude
	☐ Overall survival	☐ No overall survival
	May include	
	☐ Progression free survival ☐ Death ☐ Adverse events ☐ Quality of life	
Study design	Include	Exclude
	☐ RCT ☐ Systematic review/meta-analysis	☐ Not an RCT or systematic review/meta-analysis
Overall decision	☐ **INCLUDED**	☐ **EXCLUDED**
Notes		

screening, you don't actually have to complete the form but it is a good idea to have it to hand as you read through titles and abstracts and make decisions about the potential eligibility of individual studies.

Ideally, you and a fellow researcher (maybe your supervisor or a fellow student) will independently screen a few titles and abstracts and then meet up to compare and discuss which references each has included and excluded. This is to ensure that you both fully understand the type of studies to be included in the review. If there are any references which one of you has included and the other has not, you should discuss these discordant opinions to see whether one of you simply 'missed' it or whether there is genuine disagreement. This pilot testing reduces the chances of regular disagreements later in the review about what studies should or should not be included. As for the number of references to look at during the pilot exercise, this will depend on the number of citations you have identified. It is not uncommon for your search strategy to have identified hundreds, if not thousands, of citations, particularly in the early stages of searching. It may therefore be sensible to pilot your screening and selection tool on around 30 titles and abstracts.

Step 2   Screen all titles and abstracts identified via searches using inclusion criteria (Stage 1)

Having de-duplicated your references and piloted your screening and selection tool, the next step is to apply your inclusion criteria. Different ways in which you might develop your inclusion criteria have been discussed in Chapter 2. Applying inclusion criteria is commonly referred to as 'screening and selection' and is usually conducted in two stages (Stage 1 = screening titles and abstracts; Stage 2 = selecting full-text papers). It is considered best practice for two researchers to independently carry out the screening and selection of studies; we consider this to be essential if you are planning to publish your review. However, we realize that if you are a student working independently this might not be possible. If you are working independently then you need to state this as a limitation in the 'Discussion' section of your thesis.

Screening titles and abstracts

During screening, the identification of *potentially* relevant studies is determined solely by applying your inclusion criteria to the title and abstract of each reference that you found via searching. This stage simply entails applying your inclusion criteria to the title and abstract to determine if the study appears to meet all criteria or not. If you have any doubts about whether a reference should be included at this stage (in particular, if it is unclear if all of your inclusion criteria are met), it is always safest to include it.

You do need to scan every reference identified by your searches and this task can be time consuming; it can take days or even weeks if you have hundreds or thousands to look at. If you are working electronically, you can export your titles and abstracts into a word-processing package and then use the 'find' function to highlight relevant keywords (as bold text and/or in a different color). For example, if you are only looking for cohort studies, then you can find and highlight 'cohort' or if you are only looking for studies that include patients with low self-esteem, then you can find and highlight 'self-esteem'; this simple activity makes potentially relevant articles easier to spot. However, you will need to be creative and think outside the box about how these concepts may be described in the text to reduce your chance of excluding relevant articles by accident – electronic scanning may speed up the screening process but should never take the place of manual scanning of titles and abstracts. During this process it is also worthwhile making a note of any references that are useful and can be used to inform the background or discussion chapters of your thesis.

If there has been some delay between your scoping searches and your main search, then before you start to scan your references, it may be prudent to check whether your main search results include any relevant recently published systematic reviews that have addressed your review question. An easy way to check is to search for the words 'systematic review' in your main search results and then to scan all of the titles and abstracts where those terms appear. Such a search may be possible within your bibliographic software package or by exporting all the titles and abstracts into a word-processing package (and again highlighting the keywords 'systematic review'). If you are extremely unlucky and a review addressing your research question has been published, then revisit Chapter 2 for tips on what to do next.

Step 3   Obtain full-text papers of all potentially eligible studies

Once you have completed screening of titles and abstracts, you then need to obtain copies of the papers you marked for possible inclusion in the review. You need to have the full text of each potentially eligible reference in front of you – either electronically or in paper format. While an increasing number of full-text papers are available online, it is probable that some relevant papers are not. Your institution is likely to have an inter-library loans system and, if so, this is an obvious route for obtaining your selected papers when they are not available electronically or held in the library. Alternatively, you can try to contact authors and ask them to send or email you a copy of their publications. If, having tried all of these routes, you have been unable to obtain the full-text versions of the papers that you need, then when you write your thesis, you should clearly identify which references you have been unable to obtain as this is a limitation of your review (see Chapter 7).

Step 4   Apply inclusion criteria and select full-text papers for inclusion in the review (Stage 2)

Having obtained the full-text paper, the next step is to determine whether the paper really does meet your inclusion criteria. If it doesn't then it is important to note the reason you decided to exclude the paper at this stage. You can record which studies are to be included or excluded using the bibliographic software package in which your references are stored, or you can write up your reasons on the paper copy of your inclusion form. When you produce your full list of included studies you may find it helpful to list all of your excluded references, together with reasons for exclusion, in a table that can be placed in an Appendix of your thesis. Having a list of exclusion criteria can be helpful as it may provide you with a speedy way of excluding records without having to review them in detail. For example, you might decide to exclude all studies that include pharmaceutical interventions and include studies only looking at public health interventions. If use of pharmaceutical interventions is listed as an exclusion criterion, you can exclude these types of papers immediately without reading through the text looking for public health interventions.

As recommended in Chapter 2, it is may be worth, at this stage, emailing experts in the topic area to check that you haven't missed any relevant studies. We recommend that you are very clear in your email about what you want from them and include a set of well-defined questions to maximize your chances of a response (see Box 3.2).

Box 3.2

Example of a well thought out email

Dear Professor Smith

Re: Systematic review of non-pharmacological treatments for the management of agitation in patients with psychotic illness

I would be very grateful if you could advise me on two aspects of a review that I am currently conducting as part of my Master's studies at the University of Liverpool. I've completed my searching and have applied my inclusion criteria (please see attached). As a published expert in this clinical area, please could you have a quick read through my list of included studies and let me know if you are aware of any pertinent studies that I may have missed during my searches and/or if you know of any ongoing studies that are due to publish in the next 3 months?

Thank you very much for your help.

Yours sincerely

Student

Step 5   Report results of your searches (using PRISMA diagram)

It is important to keep detailed records of the methods that you used to search for studies and their results. Having this information available means that you (and others) can re-run and update the searches at a later date. It should also make life easier for you when it comes to writing the 'Methods' (how you searched for studies) and 'Results' (reporting the number of citations you found) sections of your thesis. You therefore need to make sure that you record the following information:

- date each search carried out;
- version of each bibliographic database searched (for example, MEDLINE 1946 to Present with Daily Update);
- interface used for each bibliographic database searched (for example, Ovid or Dialog, which can both be used to access MEDLINE);
- copies of all the search terms used for each specific search;
- number of references identified by each search;
- number of duplicates removed;

- number of references you looked at when screening titles and abstracts;
- number of references you looked at when selecting full-text papers;
- number of references you excluded at stage 2 and the reasons for exclusion.

An example of how you might report the results of your searching in the 'Results' section of your thesis is provided in the case study which is included at the end of this chapter.

You may also find it useful to read the Preferred Reporting Items for Systematic Reviews and Meta-Analyses (PRISMA) statement (Liberati et al., 2009; Moher, Liberati, Tetzlaff and Altman, 2009) before you start your review – forewarned is forearmed. PRISMA is an evidence-based minimum set of items that aims to help reviewers improve the reporting of systematic reviews and meta-analyses. The main PRISMA tool is a 27-item checklist and a four-phase flow diagram that outlines all aspects of the conduct of a systematic review (Liberati et al., 2009). Take a look at the PRISMA website; you'll find discussion documents as well as the current version of the PRISMA Statement. A template of the flow diagram which maps out the number of records identified, included and excluded, and the reasons for exclusions, is available from the website as a PDF and also as a word-processing document. A flow diagram similar to the PRISMA flow diagram should be included in the 'Results' section of your thesis. An example of a flow diagram from a systematic review is provided in Figure 3.1 as part of the case study presented at the end of the chapter.

Final thoughts

We hope that, after reading this chapter, you feel sufficiently confident to search for evidence, know who to ask for help, are able to screen titles and abstracts and select the final papers for inclusion in your review. It's worth talking to your supervisors before beginning your searches as they may be able to identify key papers in the topic area that you can use as a starting point when developing your main search. They will also be able to advise you about how much evidence you need to find, where to search for it and who, in your institution, may be able to help you search. Seeking help at this stage may save you time in the long run. Read the case study at the end of this chapter for an example of how to write up your search strategy in your thesis.

Key points to think about when writing your protocol

- Summary details of your scoping searches and results are useful to the reader;
- List the databases (and any other resources) you plan to use for your main search;
- Clearly report how you will include or exclude studies, that is, how you will screen and select the studies (and how many people will conduct these tasks) – importantly, you should include a table detailing your inclusion criteria;
- A sample search strategy in an Appendix to your protocol is helpful; for example, you could outline the search terms you plan to use for a particular database.

What an examiner is looking for in your thesis

- Sufficient detail about your search strategy so that it could, at least in theory, be replicated by another person – this requires a description of how you carried out your main search in your 'Methods' section with details of the search terms used, resources searched and date searches were carried out (usually located in an Appendix);
- Inclusion of a flow diagram similar to the PRISMA diagram in your 'Results' section;
- A brief explanation of why you excluded studies when selecting full texts.

Case study

How to report your search strategy in your 'Methods' and 'Results' sections

This case study is based on a systematic review conducted by the Liverpool Reviews and Implementation Group (Fleeman et al., 2011).

Methods

Methods for reviewing effectiveness

Evidence for the clinical effectiveness of lapatinib and trastuzumab for the first-line treatment of patients with metastatic breast cancer was assessed by conducting a systematic review of published research evidence. The review adhered to published guidance for undertaking reviews in health care (Centre for Reviews and Dissemination, 2009).

(Continued)

(Continued)

Identification of studies

RCTs were identified by searching major electronic medical databases including MEDLINE, EMBASE and the Cochrane Library. The search strategy was broad and not limited to RCTs. Information on studies in progress, unpublished research or research reported in the gray literature was sought by searching a range of relevant databases including the National Research Register and Controlled Clinical Trials. In addition, bibliographies of previous reviews and retrieved articles were searched. Further attempts to identify studies were made by contacting clinical experts and examining the reference lists of all retrieved articles.

Inclusion and exclusion criteria

Two reviewers independently screened all titles and abstracts. Full-text papers of any titles and abstracts that were considered relevant by either reviewer were obtained where possible. The relevance of each study was assessed according to the inclusion criteria stated in Table 3.6. Studies that did not meet the criteria were excluded and their bibliographic details were listed in an Appendix alongside reasons for their exclusion. Any discrepancies were resolved by consensus.

Table 3.6   Inclusion criteria

Study design	RCTs
Population(s)	Post-menopausal women with metastatic breast cancer who have not previously received treatment for metastatic disease
Intervention(s)	Lapatinib (Tyverb®/Tykerb®) Trastuzumab (Herceptin®)
Comparators	The two interventions will be compared with each other
Outcomes	At least one of the following outcomes:

- Overall survival
- Progression-free survival
- Time to progression
- Overall response rate
- Clinical benefit rate
- Adverse events
- Quality of life

Results

Quantity of research available

Electronic and hand searches identified 2228 citations, which, once duplicates were removed, left 2000 unique citations to be screened for inclusion (Figure 3.1).

Their titles and abstracts were assessed for their relevance to the review (Stage 1 screening), resulting in 20 potential citations being retained. The full texts of these citations were obtained. After applying inclusion criteria to these full-text papers (Stage 2 selection), 16 citations were excluded; four did not examine the appropriate intervention, eight did not have the specified patient population and four full-text papers could not be obtained. In addition, a further citation was identified following expert communication and included. Thus five citations were included in the systematic review.

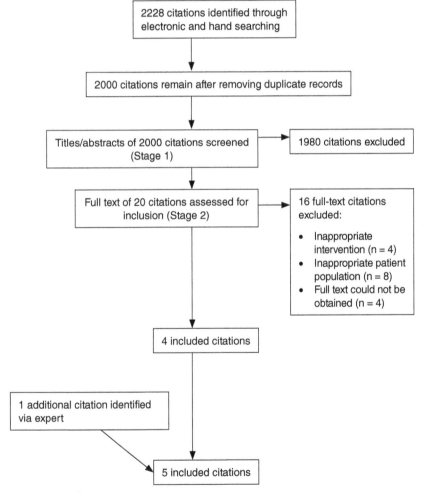

Figure 3.1 Identification of included studies in a systematic review

Frequently Asked Questions

Question 1   What if I don't have access to a librarian or
information specialist?

Input from a librarian or information specialist will help you to identify
which resources to search and how you can most effectively search them. If
you do not have access to experts, do not panic. You may find you already
have sufficient experience of using the bibliographic database that you plan
to use and your supervisor may also be able to help. It is also useful to identify systematic reviews in similar topic areas so that you can determine
which sources of data the authors searched and the search terms that they
used. Also, there are many educational resources that can help you with
your searching – from online tutorials to library information sheets (for
details see www.liv.ac.uk/systematic-review-guide).

Question 2   How can I tell if I have identified all of the relevant papers
in my search? How many studies are 'enough'?

There is no rule as to how many is 'enough'. This very much depends on
your review question and the purpose of your review. Similarly, it is impossible to be 100 per cent certain that you have identified all the relevant
papers. The important thing is that you can demonstrate that you have
searched the key resources and used an appropriate strategy to identify relevant studies. It is important to consult with others who can help, such as
an information specialist, a librarian or your supervisor.

Question 3   What if there are too many or too few studies that fulfil
my inclusion criteria?

If your search strategy retrieves too many records, you may want to refine
your inclusion criteria and modify your search terms accordingly. You
may wish to consider how you can limit your search results further, such
as by year, language or publication type (for example, journal articles,
books or letters). On the other hand, if you have only identified a small
number of studies that meet your inclusion criteria, then your search criteria may be too specific and you may wish to expand them. You may be

able to determine, from the reasons you listed when you excluded studies, which changes you need to make (for example, were the majority of studies excluded because of the study design? If so, do you want to broaden the types of included studies?). However, many credible systematic reviews have included only one study and it may be that only one study really does address your research question. However, identifying only one study may not allow you to fully demonstrate your systematic review skills to your examiner and you may wish to broaden your review question. If you do not identify any studies at all, then we suggest that you go back and modify your review question.

Question 4 **What happens if I find a useful paper that has an English abstract but the full-text paper is written in a different language?**

The first step is to determine whether the useful paper meets the inclusion criteria – typically you would look for any relevant information that is stated in the abstract. You might also think about using translation software to help you understand the methods section and any tables and figures used in the paper. Assuming that the abstract contains potentially relevant information, you have three possible options. The first is to find somebody who can translate the paper or at the very least can extract the data that you need (perhaps a fellow student). The second is to use the data from the abstract and any tables and figures that you can, noting this limitation when writing up your review. The third is to exclude this reference altogether and acknowledge this when writing the limitations of your systematic review. This last option may not be ideal, particularly if you had not stated 'English language' to be an inclusion criterion in your protocol.

4

Quality Assessment: Where Do I Begin?

Janette Greenhalgh and Tamara Brown

guide
outcomes
searches
supervisor
studies
methods
economics
protocol
research
systematic
practical
meta-analysis
quantitative
synthesis
discussion
databases
management
student
FAQ
post-graduate
review
question
qualitative
searching
quality-assessment
data
thesis

This chapter will help you to:

- identify quality assessment tool(s) that suit your review;
- carry out quality assessment of individual articles;
- tabulate and summarize the results of your quality assessment;
- think about how your quality assessment results might impact on the conclusions and recommendations of your systematic review.

Introduction

This chapter guides you as you set out to assess the quality of the studies included in your systematic review. First, we explore what we mean by quality and discuss the fundamentals of 'quality' common to all studies, regardless of study design. Second, we encourage you to think about the different types of study design that you might come across during your review, differentiating between randomized designs and non-randomized designs. Third, we emphasize how important it is to allow sufficient time to rigorously assess the quality of your included studies and discuss how the conclusions of your systematic review might be shaped by the findings of the quality assessment exercise. Finally, we encourage you to critically appraise your own systematic review using one of the many validated systematic review checklists that are available.

What is quality assessment and why do I need to do it?

By the time you reach this stage of your review you will have already identified the full set of relevant studies for inclusion in your review. Your next task is to examine the quality of each of these studies. You need to assess whether the studies have been designed, conducted and reported in such a way that they can be considered reliable (rigor) and whether or not they provide meaningful answers to your research question (relevance).

The meaning of 'quality' depends on the context in which it is used. When it comes to systematic reviewing we need to distinguish between

the quality of each of the included studies and the quality of the systematic review itself. The latter is discussed at the end of this chapter. When
used to describe a study included in a systematic review, the term 'quality'
refers to:

> The degree to which a study employs measures to minimize bias and error in its
> design, conduct and analysis. (Khan et al., 2003)

In other words, the content of the publication gives you confidence that
both its design and conduct are sufficiently robust for the results to be
trustworthy and generalizable. For example, in effectiveness studies, you
will want to be sure that the study included participants who were relevant
to the aims of the study and that sufficient numbers of participants
remained in the study to its end. To illustrate, if a study was designed to
assess the effects of reading a stop-smoking booklet on the behaviors of
adults with anxiety, the results would be of little use if the participants in
the study were adults with depression. Similarly, if only 30 out of 100 participants in the stop-smoking study were followed up and their data
included in the results, only uncertain conclusions could be reached about
the effectiveness (or otherwise) of the booklet.

If you have assessed a study as being of good or high quality, then this
is the same as saying that you are confident that the findings of the study
are credible and are highly likely to be the result of the intervention or
exposure which is being tested. Remember, it is likely that your included
studies will vary in quality. It is often mistakenly assumed that if a study
has been published in a peer-reviewed academic journal then it must be of
good quality; this is not always true. Do not take published studies at face
value. Always delve deeper and investigate your studies for flaws and
inherent weaknesses. Don't be lulled into a false sense of security by a
journal's reputation.

To illustrate, in our review of chemotherapy treatments for patients with
non-small cell lung cancer (Brown et al., 2013), we concluded that the overall quality of the 23 included studies was poor and yet these studies were all
randomized controlled trials (RCTs) published in highly regarded journals.
Similarly, one of the key points arising from our review of biofeedback for
the treatment of hypertension (Greenhalgh, Dickson and Dundar, 2009) was
that the majority of the 36 included RCTs were of such poor quality that we
were unable to synthesize the results or draw any firm conclusions from the
data available.

The advantages of quality assessing your included studies are numerous. You will develop a greater understanding of your studies and their results and you will be able to distinguish between good-quality and poor quality studies. Your review will benefit as you will be more likely to draw meaningful conclusions from the data. On a personal development level, the quality assessment exercise offers you the opportunity to acquire skills in critical appraisal.

What are the main elements of quality assessment and what do they mean?

A single quality assessment tool asks a series of questions. To be able to answer the questions, you need to think very carefully about the methods used in the studies and how the results have been reported. You must be confident that the quality assessment tool you are using measures what it purports to measure (that it is 'valid') and provides consistent results (that it is 'reliable'). Quality assessment tools ask questions about bias and it is a good idea to use tools that have been validated and checked for reliability. Examples of bias might include selection, allocation, detection, attrition and reporting bias. Common sources of bias, what bias means and the significance of each type of bias in relation to the precision of the results of a study are shown in Table 4.1. We consider that these key elements of bias are relevant to most study designs.

You may come across important issues, other than bias, that are linked to study quality. These might relate to the outcome measure employed in the study, or to the intervention itself. A number of key questions could be considered regarding the outcome measure. For example, is the outcome measure appropriate to the study? Is it a validated measure? Is it reliable? When assessing study quality it is important to consider whether the intervention was standardized across all study participants. A quality assessment tool might question this, or question whether the intervention was properly defined or described, and whether it was delivered as intended. Were those responsible for implementing the intervention appropriately trained? Finally, it might be important to assess how far the study reflects the realities of the practice being evaluated (generalizability).

Table 4.1   Important elements of quality assessment for health care intervention studies

Element	What does this mean?	Significance
Selection bias	Were the individuals selected to participate in the study likely to be representative of the target population? How were the participants selected?	You need to be able to assess how generalizable and transferable the study results are to the target population.
Allocation bias	How were participants allocated to the treatment groups? Could anyone in the study predict or control allocation to treatment groups?	Type of study design determines how participants are allocated to treatment groups; generally, the 'stronger' the study design the less risk of bias from allocation to treatment.
Performance bias	Were the participants, providers of the intervention, or the study investigators aware of the treatment that participants received or were they blinded?	You need to be able to assess whether there was awareness of treatment received by certain study personnel and whether this could bias study results.
Detection bias	Were the people who measured the study outcomes aware of what treatment participants received or were they blinded?	You need to be able to assess whether there was awareness of treatment received by study personnel and whether this could bias study results.
Attrition bias	What proportion of participants in each group stopped having the treatment? Did they stop by themselves (drop-outs) or were they stopped by study personnel (withdrawal) for whatever reason (for example, adverse event, non-compliance, did not meet inclusion criteria).	If a relatively large proportion of drop-outs occurred, this could weaken the generalizability of the study and it might also reflect that the intervention is hard to 'stick to' (it might not 'work' or it might have unpleasant side effects in the target/general population). Attrition rates can also give the reader an insight into compliance rates; if withdrawal/drop-out rates were unequal between treatment groups then this may bias the results in favor of one group.
Reporting bias	Were all outcomes stated to be measured actually reported or did the study authors fail to report outcomes which showed no (or a negative) effect? Were some results measured post hoc, that is, was an outcome measured and reported because there seemed to be a beneficial effect or perhaps the data were trawled for an 'effective' outcome?	What reasons were given to explain the failure to report all stated outcomes? The treatment may appear more favorable than it really is if negative results from other outcomes are not reported within the paper.

Element	What does this mean?	Significance
Confounders	At baseline, were the patient characteristics, such as age, sex, gender or health status, similar across all treatments?	Participants should be equally balanced in terms of variables considered important to study outcomes (for example, gender, age, health status) otherwise there is a risk that results will be biased in favor of one group/intervention.
Concurrent/ subsequent intervention	Did any of the participants receive other treatments which could have influenced the study outcomes?	Confidence that the study intervention did/did not have an effect is weakened if participants were not all treated in the same way (except for study intervention).
Analysis	Were the data for all participants included in the final analysis (even those participants who withdrew)?	If there are data missing for a number of participants and these are not accounted for, published results will not properly reflect the results of the study.
Funding bias	Who funded the study?	Funders may have a vested interest in demonstrating positive outcomes for one group/intervention.

Are any 'off the shelf' quality assessment tools available?

Don't worry, there are numerous quality assessment tools available – you don't have to design your own. There are tools that have been designed solely for the quality assessment of studies with specific types of design (for example, RCTs, cohort and cross-sectional studies) and some of these are discussed later in this chapter. There are also quality assessment tools that are designed for use with more than one study design, which can be useful if your review includes studies with a variety of designs.

Where do I start? What are the key quality assessment steps?

The six key steps of quality assessment are summarized in Table 4.2. We talk you through each step in detail.

Table 4.2   Key steps involved in quality assessment

Step 1	Note the design(s) of the studies to be included in your review
Step 2	Identify the type(s) of quality assessment tool(s) to suit your review
Step 3	Source appropriate quality assessment tool(s)
Step 4	Carry out quality assessment using the appropriate tool(s)
Step 5	Tabulate and summarize the results of your quality assessment
Step 6	Think about how the quality assessment results might impact on the recommendations and conclusions of your systematic review

Step 1   Note the design(s) of the studies to be included in your review

The first step is to identify the design(s) of your included studies so that you can choose the most appropriate quality assessment tool(s). There are different quality assessment tools available for assessing each study type. In an RCT, participants are randomly assigned to intervention groups. In non-randomized studies, participants might be allocated to different groups but not in a random manner, or the study might describe a group (or groups) of people who are either followed up over a period of time or examined at one specific point in time. Table 4.3 provides a guide to the more common study designs that you might encounter when carrying out your systematic review.

It is worth noting that, when setting inclusion criteria for a systematic review, researchers often include or exclude studies based on specific study designs. For example, often systematic reviews of the clinical effectiveness of health care interventions stipulate that only evidence from RCTs may be considered for inclusion. However, limiting inclusion criteria to specific study designs is not part of quality assessment. Quality assessment goes beyond study design. It allows you to evaluate the validity, reliability and generalizability of the results of each included study.

Step 2   Identify the type(s) of quality assessment tool(s) to suit your review

Does your systematic review include only studies of a single type of study design, or does it include a mixture of designs? If you only include one type of study, then you can use a design-specific assessment tool. If you include a range of designs, you need to decide whether to use an assessment tool for each design or an all-inclusive tool that can be used across a range of designs.

Table 4.3 Common types of study design

Design type	Description	Example
RCT	Participants are randomized to two or more treatment groups using robust methods of randomization.	The study is designed to compare the effectiveness of a new drug treatment for breast cancer with an existing drug treatment. Participants are allocated to receive their treatment via computer generated random numbers.
Non-RCT	Participants are assigned to two or more treatment groups but randomization methods are not used in the allocation process.	Participants take part in a study to assess whether cognitive behavioral therapy is more effective than drug therapy to treat anxiety. Each new participant is allocated to a treatment based on the allocation of the previous participant.
Cohort study (prospective or retrospective) May or may not include a control group	A group of participants is identified and followed over time to assess specific outcomes. There may, or may not, be a concurrent control group.	A study to assess the effects of anti-epileptic drugs on the pregnancy outcomes of women with epilepsy recruits a sample of women (via ante-natal clinics) with epilepsy who are taking anti-epileptic medication during pregnancy. A control group might be made up of women from an ante-natal clinic who have epilepsy but who are not taking anti-epileptic medication.
Case control	A group of participants with a particular condition are matched for age and other characteristics with a control group of participants who do not have the condition.	A group of children with asthma are compared with a group of children who don't have asthma. The two groups are compared in terms of birth weight to examine the influence of birth weight in the development of the condition.
Case series	A person, or series of people, who have been given a similar treatment are followed for a specific time period.	Children with autistic spectrum disorder who are given an intervention of applied behavior analysis are followed up for six months.
Cross-sectional	Data are collected from a number of people or other sources (for example, a database) at one point in time.	The relationship between intelligence and scientific reasoning in children is examined using questionnaires at one time point.

Quality assessment tools can be scales that give a numerical value of the 'quality' of a study, or they can be checklists that generate an overall picture of quality. We prefer to use a checklist rather than a scoring system as we think that a checklist provides more useful information about the quality of a study; a total quality score for a study does not provide any detail about the individual elements of the quality assessment and some individual elements of quality assessment may be more 'important' than other elements.

However, there are no hard and fast rules and the choice is yours. To read about the advantages and disadvantages of the more commonly used tools, please consult published guidance for undertaking reviews in health care (Centre for Reviews and Dissemination, 2009), or the Cochrane Handbook (Higgins and Green, 2011).

We cannot advise here on specific tools; you will need to choose the most appropriate tool for your own review. You must use the quality assessment tool in a consistent way, that is, treat all the studies the same way when assessing quality. Remember, you will need to make it clear in your protocol and thesis document how you came to select the tool you have used.

In making your decision you might want to consider a number of factors:

- Has the tool(s) been used in similar reviews in your topic area?
- A tool is often (but not always) designed and then piloted by a number of different people to test whether it measures what it is designed to measure. Has the tool been validated?
- How lengthy is the tool and how many studies do you have to quality assess? Some tools contain a considerable number of items. Are all of the items relevant to your studies? If you have included a large number of studies in your review, will you have time to use the tool on all of them?
- It can be difficult to present and succinctly discuss findings if you are using tools with a lengthy list of items, or ones that contain items requiring detailed textual responses. Is the design of the tool such that all the results are easily tabulated and simple to summarize? Will the tabulated results convey your findings efficiently?

Step 3 **Source an appropriate quality assessment tool(s)**

Take a look at other systematic reviews in the same topic area and see which tools the authors of these reviews have used. Having found some useful examples, you might then ask your supervisor if s/he can help you to determine which of these tools would be appropriate to use in your review.

In Table 4.4 we list a number of web-accessible sources of quality assessment tools. This list is not exhaustive, but is enough to help you get started. Before embarking on your search for a specific tool it is worth seeking out the recommended reporting guidelines for individual study types. These guidelines are often designed for use by journal editors and take the form of checklists to help guide decisions as to the quality of submitted articles. The Enhancing the Quality and Transparency of Health Research (EQUATOR) network website is a comprehensive source of all guidelines for health research reporting. There are guidelines for a broad range of study types; these are freely downloadable (EQUATOR, 2013). For the social scientist, the American Educational Research Association (AERA) has developed guidance for ensuring high-quality research (American Educational Research Association, 2013). We also provide a list of quality assessment tools on our website (www.liv.ac.uk/systematic-review-guide).

Table 4.4 Selected sources of quality assessment tools

Source	Contents	Our thoughts
Health Technology Assessment (HTA) report. (Deeks et al., 2003) A systematic review of quality-assessment tools for non-randomized studies. Six tools considered suitable for use in systematic reviews that included non-randomized studies. We note that the authors of the review did not consider any particular tool to be perfect.	Cowley (1995) (covers comparative and uncontrolled case series). 13-item checklist. Downs and Black (1998) (randomized and non-randomized studies). 27-item checklist. Newcastle-Ottawa scale (Wells et al., 2012) (cohort and case control studies). 8-item checklist. Reisch (any study design). 34 'key' item checklist. Thomas (no date) (any study design). 21-item checklist. Zaza et al. (2000) (any study design). 22-item checklist.	These tools were considered suitable for use in systematic reviews by the authors of the HTA report.
Critical Appraisal Skills Programme (CASP) (CASP, 2013)	Critical appraisal checklists for RCTs, systematic reviews, cohorts, case controls.	These checklists were designed to help clinicians assess evidence and so some items may not be relevant to your systematic review.
The Cochrane Handbook (Higgins and Green, 2011)	The 'risk of bias' tool used for RCTs in Cochrane reviews. The Cochrane Group are piloting a new tool for assessing the risk of bias in non-randomized studies.	Detailed approach to quality assessment; time consuming to use but very informative if applied conscientiously.
Centre for Reviews and Dissemination guidance (Centre for Reviews and Dissemination, 2009)	Guidance for conducting systematic reviews in health care.	Contains guides to criteria important in the assessment of studies. We use a slightly modified version of this guidance in many of our reviews.
Social Care Institute for Excellence (SCIE) (Social Care Institute for Excellence, 2010)	Guidelines for conducting systematic reviews in social care.	Offers guidelines on the minimum generic criteria for quality assessing empirical studies.

Step 4   Carry out quality assessment using the appropriate tool

In the context of your review, it is up to you *when* you carry out the quality assessment exercise; you can do it before, during or after data extraction. If you are extracting study data before you carry out your quality assessment, you are blind to study quality and your reporting will not be biased. However, if you are intending to exclude poor quality studies from your review, then you need to carry out your quality assessment before extracting data. If you choose to assess study quality after you have extracted data your greater familiarity with the study may help you to answer the quality assessment questions.

Once you have chosen an appropriate quality assessment tool it is time to pilot the tool. Piloting in this context just means testing the tool to see if it 'works' by taking one or two studies and seeing if you can answer the quality assessment questions. If you are working with a colleague, then you can both be involved in piloting the tool.

When you are confident that you are both using the tool in the same way then you should both (independently) answer the quality assessment questions for each of the studies or one of you can cross-check the quality assessment responses of the other reviewer; again, working with a colleague on this task is essential if you are planning to publish your review. After completing quality assessment you need to compare your responses and discuss any differences. If any issues remain unresolved (despite several cups of coffee), try to find a third person to resolve the outstanding issues.

Should you find yourself working on your own, it might be useful to compare your quality assessment results with any published critiques of your included studies that are available in the public domain. Do be sure to note in your 'Discussion' section why, and how, the absence of a second reviewer to quality assess your included studies is a limitation of your systematic review.

We recommend that you keep careful notes about your decisions and consistently mark the text of the paper where you found information – marking can be carried out on paper or electronically.

Quality assessment of randomized controlled trials

The RCT is considered to be at the top of the evidence hierarchy in terms of design quality. Table 4.5 shows a tool that can be used to quality assess RCTs. We have designed this tool using the quality assessment criteria for RCTs recommended by the CRD (Centre for Reviews and Dissemination, 2009). Note that the list includes questions relating to the quality criteria previously described in Table 4.1. When using this tool you should complete the checklist for each included study. The responses are limited to Yes/No/Partially/Not stated/Not applicable. You can add further columns to the right-hand side of your table to allow space for all studies included in your review. At the end of the exercise you will be able to visually compare the studies by each item or component of the assessment.

Table 4.5   Example tool for quality assessment of randomized controlled trials

Reviewer name:
Author name/Study ID:
Quality item
Randomization (check for allocation bias)
Was the method used to assign participants to the treatment groups truly random?
Was the allocation of treatment concealed?
Was the number of participants randomized stated?
Comparability (check for confounding)
Were details of baseline comparability presented?
Was baseline comparability achieved?
Eligibility (check for selection bias)
Were eligibility criteria for study entry specified?
Were there any co-interventions that may influence outcomes for each group?
Blinding (check for detection bias)
Were outcome assessors blinded to treatment allocation?
Were the individuals who administered the intervention blinded to treatment allocation?
Were participants blinded to treatment allocation?
Was the success of the blinding procedures assessed?
Withdrawals (check for attrition bias)
Were ≥ 80% of participants randomized included in the final analysis?
Were reasons for participant withdrawals stated?
Were there any unexpected drop-outs in either group?
Was an intention to treat analysis included?
Outcomes (check for outcome reporting bias)
Is there evidence that more outcomes were measured than were reported?

However, as we noted earlier (and will become apparent later in this chapter), RCTs can be poorly executed and open to the influence of bias. Not all studies can be RCTs. Many areas of research do not lend themselves well to being examined using RCT methodology due to the nature of the research question and/or the intervention of interest. In addition, ethical and/or financial reasons can make it problematic or inappropriate to carry out a RCT.

Quality assessment of non-randomized studies

As noted earlier, many elements of quality assessment are common to all types of study design. Studies other than RCTs are also open to specific types of bias and so the measure of quality assessment for your review needs to include items to account for these additional concerns. These concerns may include, but are not limited to questions about:

- relevance of the research design to the research question;
- representativeness of the study participants to the research question;
- how participants were recruited;
- whether any comparison groups were utilized;
- how many people started the study and how many remained at the end;
- whether the measurement tools used in the study were valid, reliable and relevant.

In this section we present the Newcastle-Ottawa Scale (NOS) for assessing cohort studies (Wells et al., 2012). This scale is widely used and often modified to suit the needs of individual reviews. For example, colleagues at the University of Liverpool have adapted the NOS to appraise included studies in their review (Pope et al., 2010). There are tailored versions of the NOS for cohort studies (Box 4.1), case–control studies, intervention studies and cross-section studies.

Box 4.1

Newcastle-Ottawa Quality Assessment Scale: Cohort Studies

Note: The tool uses a 'star system' by which a study is judged on three broad perspectives: the selection of the study groups; the comparability of the groups; and the ascertainment of either the exposure or outcome of interest for case–control or cohort studies respectively. Stars are pre-awarded in the NOS and are used to indicate quality elements. A study can be awarded a maximum of one star for each numbered item within the Selection and Outcome categories. A maximum of two stars can be given for Comparability. The handbook for interpretation of the NOS is available at www.ohri.ca/programs/clinical_epidemiology/oxford.asp.

Selection:

1) Representativeness of the exposed cohort

   a) truly representative of the average _____ (describe) in the community*
   b) somewhat representative of the average _____ in the community*
   c) selected group of users, for example, nurses, volunteers
   d) no description of the derivation of the cohort

2) Selection of the non-exposed cohort

   a) drawn from the same community as the exposed cohort*
   b) drawn from a different source
   c) no description of the derivation of the non-exposed cohort

3) Ascertainment of exposure

   a) secure record (for example, surgical records)*
   b) structured interview*
   c) written self-report
   d) no description

4) Demonstration that outcome of interest was not present at start of study

   a) yes*
   b) no

Comparability:

1) Comparability of cohorts on the basis of the design or analysis

   a) study controls for _____ (select the most important factor)*
   b) study controls for any additional factor* (this criterion could be modified to indicate specific control for a second important factor)

Outcome:

1) Assessment of outcome

   a) independent blind assessment*
   b) record linkage*
   c) self-report
   d) no description

(Continued)

(Continued)

2) Was follow-up long enough for outcomes to occur

    a) yes (select an adequate follow up period for outcome of interest)*
    b) no

3) Adequacy of follow up of cohorts

    a) complete follow up – all subjects accounted for*
    b) subjects lost to follow-up unlikely to introduce bias – small number lost
        – > ____ % (select an adequate %) follow up, or description provided of
        those lost)*
    c) follow up rate < ____% (select an adequate %) and no description of
        those lost
    d) no statement

Reproduced with permission from Professor George A. Wells, University of Ottawa
Heart Institute

Quality assessment of systematic reviews

If your searches have identified published systematic reviews in your topic area,
you may want to use them as a reference tool. First, their reference lists make it
easy for you to check that you haven't missed any potentially relevant studies.
Second, reading the background and conclusion sections means that you can
very quickly identify any important potential issues that you might also wish to
consider in your review. When conducting our systematic review of biofeedback
for the treatment of hypertension (Greenhalgh et al., 2009), we found two existing systematic reviews in the same topic area. This was fine as our task was to
critique and update one of these. As part of the background section to our review
we provided a quality assessment of the existing reviews and we also used these
reviews as a check for relevant papers. In our systematic review of clopidogrel
and modified-release dipyridamole for the prevention of occlusive vascular
events (Greenhalgh et al., 2011), we found several existing systematic reviews;
however, none addressed the specific question of interest in our review. In this
case, we used the existing reviews to check for potentially relevant papers and
provided a quality assessment of each systematic review in the Appendix of our
report to demonstrate that we were aware of their existence.

It may be useful to apply a systematic review assessment tool to your work
as a final check of your report. Your supervisor and/or examiner might also use
a tool for this purpose. Table 4.6 is an example of a quality assessment tool

Table 4.6   Quality assessment of systematic reviews

Reviewer name:
Author name/Study ID:
Quality item
Response: Yes/No/Partially/Not stated/Not applicable

Was the review question clearly defined in terms of population, interventions, comparators, outcomes and study designs?
Was the search strategy adequate and appropriate?

Were there any restrictions on language, publication status or publication date?
Were preventative steps taken to minimize bias and errors in the study selection process?
Were appropriate criteria used to assess the quality of the primary studies, and were preventative steps taken to minimize bias and errors in the quality assessment process?
Were preventative steps taken to minimize bias and errors in the data extraction process?
Were adequate details presented for each of the primary studies?
Were appropriate methods used for data synthesis?

Were differences between studies assessed?

Were the studies pooled, and if so was it appropriate and meaningful to do so?
Do the authors' conclusions accurately reflect the evidence that was reviewed?

suitable for use with systematic reviews. This was adapted from the guidance document produced by the CRD (Centre for Reviews and Dissemination, 2009).

Step 5   **Tabulate and summarize the results of your quality assessment**

Now is the time to summarize your quality assessment findings by tabulating the results and describing them in your text. The quality assessment section is typically presented within the 'Results' section of a review, immediately after the text that states how many studies were identified and immediately before tables describing study characteristics and patient characteristics.

In Table 4.7 we present an example of a quality assessment table that appears in our systematic review of first-line chemotherapy treatments for non-small cell lung cancer (Brown et al., 2013). The review included 23 RCTs but here, for brevity, we only show the results for the first 15 studies. We order the studies in the table by date, but you can order them in other ways, for example, alphabetically by first author. No matter how you plan to order your studies in your tables, remember to use this order consistently in all of the tables throughout your review.

Information in Table 4.7 shows that the studies differed in terms of their quality. Even though these were all RCTs published in peer-reviewed journals, nine of the 15 studies failed to report important information describing

Table 4.7 Example of quality assessment table of randomized controlled trials

Trial	Randomization			Baseline comparability		Inclusion criteria specified	Co-interventions identified	Blinding				Withdrawals		Intention to treat	Other outcomes
	Truly random	Allocation concealment	Number stated	Presented	Achieved			Assessors	Administration	Participants	Procedure assessed	<80% in final analysis	Reasons stated		
Chen (2004)	NS	NS	✓	✓	✓	✓	✓	NS	NS	NS	NS	✓	✓	✓	✗
Chen (2007)	NS	✓	✓	✓	✓	✓	✓	NS	NS	NS	NS	✓	✓	✓	✗
Douillard (2005)	NS	NS	✓	✓✗	NS	✓	✓	NS	NS	NS	NS	✓	✓	✓	✓
Fossella (2003)	NS	✓	✓	✓	✓	✓	✓	✗	✗	✗	NA	✓	✓	✓	✗
Gebbia (2003)	NS	✓	✓	✓	NS	✓	✓	NS	NS	NS	NS	✓	✓	✓	✗
Gridelli (2003)	✓	✓	✓	✓	NS	✓	✓	NS	NS	NS	NS	✓	✓	✓	✗
Helbekkmo (2007)	✓	✓	✓	✓✗	✓	✓	✓	NS	NS	NS	NS	✓	✓	✗	✗
Kelly (2001)	NS	NS	✓	✓	NS	✓	NS	NS	NS	NS	NS	✓	✓	✗	✓
Langer (2007)	✓	NS	✓	✓	NS	✓	NS	NS	NS	NS	NS	✓	✓	✓	✗
Martoni (2005)	NS	NS	✓	✓	NS	✓	✓	NS	NS	NS	NS	✓	✓	✗	✗
Ohe (2007)	✓	✓	✓	✓	NS	✓	✓	NS	NS	NS	NS	✓	✓	✗	✗
Scagliotti (2002)	✓	✓	✓	✓✗	NS	✓	✓	NS	NS	NS	NS	✓	✓	✗	✗
Schiller (2002)	NS	NS	✓	✓	NS	✓	✓✗	NS	NS	NS	NS	✓	✓	✗	✗
Smit (2003)	✓	NS	✓	✓	NS	✓	✓	NS	NS	NS	NS	✓	✓	✗	✗
Thomas (2006)	NS	NS	✓	✓	✓✗	✓	NS	✗	✗	✗	NA	✓	✓	✗	✗

✓ yes (item adequately addressed); ✗ no (item not adequately addressed); ✓✗ partially (item partially addressed); NS not stated; NA not applicable the details of the methods used to randomize participants to treatment arms. In addition, ten of the studies did not state whether the participants in each treatment arm were balanced in terms of their personal characteristics (for example, similar numbers of males and females in each arm, participants were of a similar age). In the overall summary of the quality of the 23 studies included in our review we concluded that:

> Overall methodological quality of included studies was poor. Only six of the 23 included studies reported sufficient information for them to be assessed as adequately randomized and with adequate concealment of allocation. All studies clearly reported the number of participants randomized. All studies reported inclusion criteria and, with the exception of four studies, all reported details about co-interventions, for example palliative radiotherapy and/or second-line chemotherapy. Six studies were reported as 'open'. Blinding of participants, investigators or outcome assessors was considered to be not stated in 16 out of the 23 included studies. The outcomes of over 80 per cent of patients were assessed in all studies and all studies reported reasons for drop-out; ten trials used an intention to treat approach to assess overall survival. Five of the studies appeared to report fewer outcomes than initially stated. (Brown et al., 2013)

Step 6 Think about how the quality assessment results might impact on the conclusions and recommendations of your systematic review

Now that you have tabulated and summarized the results of the quality assessment exercise, you should have a good overview of your included studies. You should now start to think about how the quality of your studies might impact on the credibility of the overall results of your systematic review. Irrespective of which tool you use to assess your studies, you need to summarize the findings in your thesis. You could use previous reviews in the topic area to guide you when you come to write up your quality assessment exercise. To help you, also look for any guidance notes that accompany the quality assessment tool that you have used. Think about what you, as a reader, might want to know about the results of the quality assessment. Does the summary allow other readers to reach an informed conclusion about the quality of the studies included in your review? Remember, you should only present the results of your quality assessment exercise in the 'Results' section; save discussion of these findings for the 'Discussion' section of your thesis.

Final thoughts

We have summarized the key points from this chapter in Box 4.2. Although you should save discussion of your results for the 'Discussion' section of your thesis, we considered it appropriate to finish this chapter with a few pointers to help you formulate your discussion:

- Were you surprised by the results of the quality assessment exercise? Did you find any elements of the exercise noteworthy?
- Did any of the results from individual studies appear to be different to the majority of study results? Were any specific quality issues associated with these studies?
- How should the study results be synthesized? Is it reasonable to 'lump' similar study interventions together if quality differs markedly between studies? If the majority of studies included in your systematic review are assessed as being of poor quality then you need to consider whether or not to carry out a meta-analysis. If you are planning to meta-analyze study results, should a sensitivity analysis of study results based on quality also be undertaken (see Chapter 6)? For example, excluding poor-quality studies may change outliers and effect size and/or confidence intervals around the effect size.
- Did you find any patterns across studies? Can you offer recommendations for future research? For example, did the majority of your included studies fail to describe how participants were selected? A recommendation for future research could then include a statement that any future studies relevant to the topic of your review must improve the reporting of participant selection as this would enable reviewers to assess the generalizability of the study results to the target population.

For other ideas on how to integrate and discuss your quality assessment findings in your review, look at other reviews in your subject area and read Chapter 7.

Box 4.2

'Top Tips' for quality assessment

- ✓ Quality assessment can be a time consuming process and should not be left until the last minute.
- ✓ Carefully document where in the study you found information relating to each quality assessment question. This can save time later on and prevent you from having to rely on memory if you have to go back and check your reasoning.

✓ Use footnotes beneath the quality assessment table to clarify your responses where necessary. For example, if the participant characteristics were partially comparable between the groups, you might want to say in a footnote that this was because there were more males in one group than in another. As well as guiding the reader, this will help you when writing up the results.

✓ Make notes of anything which stands out as 'interesting' or 'quirky' when you quality assess a study as this can help jog your memory of the study characteristics and help you to make sense of the study results.

✓ Quality assessing a paper appears to be a straightforward matter of answering a list of questions. However, the task is rarely so black and white. Whichever tool you use, some degree of subjective judgment will be required to enable you to answer some of the questions. This is why it is useful to have a second reviewer to quality assess your studies.

✓ Keep records of how you came to make your decisions, especially when you were unable to give a clear 'yes' or 'no' response to a question.

✓ Sometimes it may not be clear to you what a quality assessment question is really asking, even when there is a guide to help you use the tool. If this is the case, discuss your concerns with your peers or supervisor.

✓ Reviewer experience, in terms of the topic being studied and familiarity with study design, can influence an individual's ability to quality assess studies. Ideally each included study should be quality assessed by two reviewers independently.

Key points to think about when writing your protocol

- Types of studies (for example, randomized or non-randomized) that you intend to include in your review;
- Quality assessment strategy (for example, what tool will you use, when will you use it and will anyone help you?);
- Length of time you plan to spend on the exercise.

What an examiner is looking for in your thesis

- Appropriate use of quality assessment tool(s) and a list of their associated strengths and weaknesses;
- Summary and tabulation of the results of your quality assessment exercise;
- Detailed reporting of your quality assessment findings;
- Clear discussion of how the quality assessment results might link to the review conclusions.

Frequently Asked Questions

Question 1   How long does quality assessment take?

Key steps include reading the publication(s), reading through the appropriate quality assessment tool, completing the tool, writing up the results in the review and synthesizing your results with the effectiveness data. Usually, it will take *at least* 45 minutes to complete a quality assessment tool for one study publication. Quality assessment is not a quick task. You need to allow sufficient time to carry it out properly.

Question 2   How do I quality assess a study that is reported in more than one paper?

If a study is reported in more than one paper then you should treat the paper with the key study data as the 'core' paper using the other papers as supplements. The 'core' paper would be used in the quality assessment exercise. It is advisable for you to read all of the papers relating to the study, especially if you are unclear about any of the study methods. If, for example, you can only answer a question using data presented in a supplement then you will need to add in a footnote to your quality assessment table to explain the source of this information. If, for reasons of time (or finances), you cannot obtain all of the papers you should acknowledge this in the limitations of your review.

Question 3   How do I (and should I) assess the quality of an abstract?

If you have included abstracts in your review (for example, from a conference, or from a non-English-language paper with an English abstract), these should be quality assessed as far as is possible. It should be made clear in the quality assessment table (using a footnote) and in the summary text that the study data were only available from an abstract. If there is missing or unclear information, the reader will then be aware that the study information was limited rather than assume that it came from a poor quality study.

Question 4 How do I deal with a very poor quality study?

You should highlight any poor quality studies in your write up of the quality assessment exercise. You should also consider their impact on the overall results of the review. If you are planning to conduct a meta-analysis, consider carrying out a sensitivity analysis (see Chapter 6) in which poor-quality studies are excluded.

Question 5 Why should I bother quality assessing studies?

Whilst quality assessment might seem like a tick-box exercise, it is an important step in any systematic review. The important part is linking the results of the quality assessment with the conclusions of your review. Quality assessment isn't just limited to students undertaking postgraduate theses: many important bodies in the field of (public) health now include 'evidence statements' or 'evidence summaries' alongside advice and recommendations in their reports. For example, the National Institute for Health and Care Excellence (NICE) uses evidence statements to reflect the strength of the evidence which is derived from a synthesis of the quality, quantity and consistency of the evidence gathered from carrying out reviews (National Institute for Health and Clinical Excellence, 2009). Quality assessment results are an important element underpinning the strength of the evidence, and can be used to help experts formulate and prioritize recommendations for practice. Further, the Cochrane Collaboration has recently introduced Summary of Findings (SoF) tables for each systematic review (Higgins and Green, 2011). Similar to NICE's evidence statements, the purpose of the SoF table is to help improve decision making and increase the usability of Cochrane Reviews. Like the NICE evidence statements, a key part of the SoF table is quality assessment of the included evidence. These two practical examples show the importance of quality assessment in informing evidence (or study results) that is used to change practice.

5

Data Extraction: Where Do I Begin?

Nigel Fleeman and Yenal Dundar

guide
outcomes
searches
methods
supervisor
studies
economics
protocol
research
systematic
practical
meta-analysis
quantitative
synthesis
student
discussion
databases
management
FAQ
post-graduate
review
question
qualitative
searching
quality-assessment
data
thesis

This chapter will help you to:

- understand the purpose of data extraction;
- decide when to undertake your data extraction;
- store the data you have extracted;
- feel confident about reporting the results of your data extraction.

Introduction

This chapter has been written to guide you through the process of data extraction and to encourage you to think about the links between data extraction, data presentation, data tables and data synthesis. Guidance on what data to extract and how and where data should be stored is also provided. In addition, we discuss the best time to complete the data extraction exercise.

What do we mean by data extraction?

By this stage in the review process you will have already identified which papers contain evidence to help you answer your review question. You have probably completed your quality assessment exercise and are becoming familiar with the data within your included studies. Your next step is to identify, and then extract, relevant data from each individual study. Data extraction is the process whereby relevant data are taken from your included papers and stored in one single format, that is, in a data extraction form. We recommend that you use a bespoke data extraction form. Within your thesis, you need to present your data in the data extraction tables that you have designed. This process allows you (and the reader of your thesis) to make sense of the data, both descriptively and analytically.

Table 5.1 outlines the key steps involved in extracting data from studies.

Table 5.1   Key steps to consider when extracting data from studies

Step 1	Identify the data that you want to extract
Step 2	Build (and pilot) your data extraction form and data extraction tables
Step 3	Set out plans for working with others (if appropriate)
Step 4	Decide when you are going to carry out the data extraction and where you will store the extracted data
Step 5	Complete your data extraction tables
Step 6	Report your extracted data in your thesis

Step 1 Identify the data that you want to extract

The purpose of data extraction is to present information to help you answer your review question. Therefore, before extracting any data, it is worth re-reading your protocol and review question. Your review protocol will be useful to you as you should have already described your plans for data extraction.

It may be a good idea to skim read all of your included papers at this stage as this will allow you to gain a sense of the data within the studies. The data that you extract and the data tables that you include in your thesis should provide an overview of all of the data from your included studies. Early in the review process, it is a good idea to list the different types of data that you think you will need to help you to summarize, describe and interpret the results of your included studies, both as individual studies and as a collection of studies.

When carrying out a systematic review you are primarily interested in two types of data: descriptive data (for example, study characteristics) and analytical data (for example, outcomes). You might also want to have a look at published reviews in the same topic area as your review to help you identify specific data that you want to extract.

It is a good idea to err on the side of caution and extract more, rather than less, data as it is easier to delete data than go back to studies later to collect more data. However, you need to be careful and make sure that you only extract data that are likely to be useful and will help you to address your research question. For example, while data on the ethnicity of the participants in a study may be useful to answer some review questions, such data may not be relevant to other review questions.

Step 2   Build (and pilot) your data extraction form and data
extraction tables

Once you have decided on the data that you want to extract, you can start
to put together your data extraction form and think about how you will
build your data extraction tables. If you have well-designed data extraction forms then you are less likely to have to keep returning to the source
paper(s) of each individual study during the review process. Whether you
design a form using a software package or plain, old-fashioned paper is
up to you. To ensure that data extraction errors are minimized, sometimes data are extracted from studies by two independent reviewers and
then cross-checked. If you are using this approach, just remember to
make sure that it is your data extraction that ends up in the tables of your
thesis. Or, more typically, data are extracted by one reviewer and simply
checked for accuracy by a second reviewer thus saving time and money.
When extracting data it is a good idea to record where in the full-text
paper the extracted data are located. One way to do this is to highlight
the extracted data in the original study (electronic or paper version). This
is particularly helpful if a second reviewer is going to cross-check your
data extraction.

It is not uncommon to discover that a study has been published in multiple publications, often with different outcomes reported in each, or the
same outcomes reported at different time points. When this is the case, it is
best practice to consider all of the different sources as one paper and to
extract all of the data on the same form. Where the data differ across publications, this should be noted and, if possible, investigated.

It is never too early to start thinking about how your data extraction tables
will look in your thesis. You should (ideally) be aware of potential stylistic
differences between papers. For example, a mean and standard deviation
may be presented as '64 (12)' in one paper and '64 ± 12' in another. You
need to decide how you want to record these data in your data extraction
form. While it is not essential to be stylistically consistent at this stage, you
can save yourself a great deal of time and effort by deciding now, before the
review progresses further, how you want to present the data in the tables of
your thesis.

It is a good idea to pilot your data extraction form using at least two or
three of your included studies. As with other stages in the systematic review,

piloting your data extraction form can save a lot of time and energy if done early on in the review process. The aims of the pilot exercise are twofold: first, to ascertain how easy it is to extract the data; and, second, to check whether all the necessary data are being captured. Piloting should prevent problems such as making the late discovery that important data have not been extracted. You may find that, at the piloting stage, you need to add or remove variables from your form.

Step 3 Set out plans for working with others (if appropriate)

If more than one person is extracting data, then piloting your data extraction form will include a check on whether both reviewers share the same understanding of the form and the data. For example, age is likely to be an important variable for most studies; when extracting data on age, you need to ensure that you explicitly state on your form whether you are referring to mean or median, standard deviation or range, and so on.

Again, if more than one person is extracting data, then the extracted datasets need to be compared (cross-checked) and there may be occasions when you and your fellow reviewer do not agree about the data you have extracted. Hopefully, most disagreements can be resolved through discussion. You may disagree because the data in the original study are misleading, for example, data contained in a figure or table do not appear to match that quoted in the text. Hence it is useful to note precisely from where you have extracted data to allow discrepancies to be quickly and easily rectified. Where similar issues recur for the same variable in more than one study, the disagreement may highlight issues about your review aims and/or research question that need addressing; for example, are your aims and objectives clear? Alternatively, disagreement may occur simply because of a poorly designed data extraction form, emphasizing the need for further piloting. In some situations you and the second reviewer may not be able to agree on which data should be extracted. In this case, we recommend that you obtain the opinion of a third person, perhaps your supervisor (if they are not the second reviewer), who is familiar with systematic reviews and is fully aware of the aims of your review.

However, if you are working independently you need to be creative and identify ways to ensure that the data you have extracted are accurate and complete. For example, you may be able to ask your supervisor to cross-check a sample of your data extraction. Or, you might have to put your data aside for a week or so and then redo your data extraction, cross-checking that both sets of extracted data are the same. The latter approach can be tedious but might help you to identify data extraction errors or inconsistencies.

Contacting study authors for missing or additional data

Where appropriate, contacting authors for further information and clarification can improve the quality of your review. However you should check that there are no other publications that you might have missed from your search that contain the data that you are looking for – perhaps a study was published after your search was completed. When requesting data from authors, it is important to be as clear as possible about the nature of the data you require. For example, is it a mean or median value you need? Or, is it both? It is a good idea to send the relevant part(s) of the data extraction form to the author for him/her to complete. Finally, you should prepare yourself for the fact that not all authors will respond to your data requests. It is acceptable to re-contact authors who do not respond to your first contact. It is also a good idea to log all correspondence so that when writing up your review, you can detail where you contacted an author but did not receive a response.

Step 4   Decide when you are going to carry out your data extraction and where you will store the extracted data

Whether or not you extract data before, during or after quality assessment is up to you – as is the order in which you describe what you have done in your thesis. It is sometimes recommended that data extraction takes place after the methodological quality assessment of your included studies has been carried out; this is imperative if you are planning to exclude poor-quality studies from your review (this is discussed in relation to meta-analysis in Chapter 6).

You can extract data electronically or you can extract data by hand. If you are extracting data from an electronic version of a study (such as a PDF) then it is likely that you will simply copy and paste relevant sections or chunks of data into your data extraction forms. This approach not only saves time but reduces the chances of data-entry errors. In addition, storing data electronically enables you to make, and save, backups of your work and may also make your life simpler when it comes to data synthesis. For example, some software packages enable you to analyze your data qualitatively (for example, use of a word processor or specialist software such as NVivo to move and code data) or quantitatively (for example, use of a spreadsheet package to carry out mathematical and statistical tasks).

Chapter 10 outlines the advantages and disadvantages of using different software packages for storing data. Your choice will depend, to some extent, on the amount of data you need to collect and also on your own competence and familiarity with different software packages.

Step 5   Complete your data extraction tables

After you have extracted your data, the next step is to build the data extraction tables that you will present, and then refer to, in your thesis. At this stage you should also be thinking about how you will describe and summarize the data in your thesis. All of the data discussed in your thesis are likely to be presented in tables. We cannot tell you exactly how to build your data extraction tables, but we can suggest that you try to include tables with the following headings and variables: *study characteristics* (for example, study name, identify whether full paper or abstract, type of study, intervention/ exposure, study population, country, follow-up, outcomes, study sponsorship); *participant characteristics* (for example, mean age, gender, specific participant characteristics of interest) and *study results* (for example, primary outcomes, secondary outcomes). See Chapter 6 for a more detailed discussion of the use of numerical data in your review.

Remember, a well-designed data extraction form will make it easy to produce these tables. Again, it is a good idea to look at published systematic reviews in a similar topic area to get ideas about what you should include in your tables.

Step 6   Report your extracted data in your thesis

Having extracted your data and built your tables, the next task is to report and make sense of the data. You need to report them in such a way that the reader can understand and follow your train of thought. The term 'narrative synthesis' is used to describe this process. Narrative synthesis simply refers to any presentation of results using words only (with reference to the data in tables). However, there is no point in simply repeating the data from your tables in your text – don't waste your words, or more importantly, don't annoy your examiner through repetition of data. Always use the tables to describe your data and use the text to report the overall findings. All discussion and interpretation of the data should take place in the 'Discussion' and 'Conclusions' sections of your review. Don't feel that you have to comment on everything; tables may include data not described in the accompanying text, but which nevertheless help the reader interpret individual study results and compare and contrast the included studies.

It is common practice to begin by presenting a summary of descriptive data for all of the included studies in a series of tables. The usual practice is to split the descriptive data over two tables: study characteristics and participant characteristics. To some extent, this will depend on the number of variables that you are considering. You can then go on to present the results of your included studies.

All data presented in tables should be accompanied by explanatory summary text. It is important to check that what you write in the text corresponds exactly with the information that you present in the tables. Let's assume that Table 5.2 shows the study characteristics of five hypothetical studies that can be used to assess the clinical effectiveness of catheters to prevent infection. The study characteristics table might be accompanied by the following explanatory summary text:

The five studies were carried out between 1990 and 2002. The publication dates ranged from 1993 to 2005. The trials were conducted in various countries: one in the USA, two in France and two in the UK. Three studies were carried out in an intensive care unit, one in a general hospital ward and the authors of one study did not state the setting. Commercial research support for the trial was acknowledged in three of the five trials.

Table 5.2   Example of a study characteristics table

Study	When trial conducted	Country	Trial setting	Commercial research support
Clarke (1993)	1990	USA	Intensive care unit	Not stated
Jones (1996)	1992–1993	France	Not stated	Arrow International
Radebe (2005)	2001–2002	UK	Intensive care unit	Donation by Arrowgard
Strummer (1996)	1993–1994	France	General hospital ward	Not stated
Yeboah (1998)	1995–1996	UK	Intensive care unit	Medical Kit, UK

Table 5.3 Example of a study results summary table

Study	Outcome (survival)	Age	Summary of findings (adjusted HR)
Bremner (2010)	Time from registration to death from any cause	> 65	HR = 1.15; 95% CI: 0.78 to 1.61; $p = 0.32$
Charles (2009)	Time from surgery to death from any cause	> 65	HR = 1.75; 95% CI: 0.78 to 3.51; $p = 0.11$
Strachan (1992)	Time from registration to death from any cause	> 65	HR = 1.39; 95% CI: 0.93 to 2.26; $p = 0.22$
Springsteen (2006)	Time from diagnosis to death or last contact	≤ 65	HR = 0.79; 95% CI: 0.42 to 1.71; $p = 0.51$

HR = hazard ratio; CI = confidence interval

Let's assume that Table 5.3 presents the results of four hypothetical studies that assessed the clinical effectiveness of different chemotherapy treatments for women with breast cancer. The study results table might be accompanied by the following explanatory text:

> While three of the studies (all with similar cohort characteristics) presented a hazard ratio suggesting a slight increase in overall survival for older women, the remaining study suggested an improved outcome for younger women; none of the differences were statistically significant.

Your explanatory text should also highlight any key differences in values reported by different studies; this will entail examining your tables for similarities and differences, both descriptive (for example, similar proportions of males and females) and analytical (for example, differences in magnitude or direction of reported outcomes). For example, inclusion and exclusion criteria should be similar across studies so as to be relatively confident that studies are recruiting similar types of subjects.

Beyond narrative synthesis

As previously mentioned, narrative synthesis refers to any write up of results using words only (with reference to data in tables). However, after examining your data, you might also want to investigate your data using quantitative synthesis (for example, meta-analysis); if so, please read Chapter 6 for more information. It is important to remember that a narrative synthesis of data is often sufficient. Although we encourage you to consider whether your data lend themselves to meta-analysis, a systematic review does not necessarily require one. Don't be concerned if your data are not appropriate for combination in a meta-analysis; just include an explanation in your thesis which justifies your decision.

How will you discuss the implications of the findings in your review?

After you narratively synthesize your data, you should have an idea of the similarities and differences in the results of your included studies and feel confident about discussing the implications of these results in your 'Discussion' and 'Conclusions' sections. As with quality assessment, you should only present (not discuss) your results in the 'Results' section. You now need to think about how the results of your included studies fit together and how you might structure your arguments in the 'Discussion' and 'Conclusions' sections of your thesis.

Final thoughts

To round off the chapter, we considered it appropriate to give you a few pointers on how to discuss your results in your 'Discussion' section. You may wish to consider one or several of the following:

- Were you surprised by the results of the data extraction exercise? Did you find any specific elements of the exercise noteworthy?
- Did any of the results from a single study appear to be different to the majority of the other results and, if so, did you explain why this might have occurred?
- How did you synthesize your study results? Did you carry out a meta-analysis? What were your reasons for or against using such an approach?
- Were you able to answer your review question? Did the data from your included studies have relevance to your target audience?
- Were you able to offer recommendations for future research?

For other ideas on how to integrate and discuss the findings of your review, look at published reviews in your topic area and read Chapter 7.

Key points to think about when writing your protocol

- State how many people will undertake the data extraction;
- Where more than one person will undertake the data extraction, describe how disagreements will be resolved;
- It is a good idea to state the types of data you plan to extract;
- Set a deadline for obtaining studies in the review;
- Outline your plans for piloting the data extraction form;
- Discuss your plans for narrative synthesis and meta-analysis.

What an examiner is looking for in your thesis

- Expansion of the data extraction methods described in your protocol;
- Inclusion of your data extraction form in an Appendix;
- Clearly presented tables describing key data including consistent use of headings and informative legends;
- Succinct reporting of data from included studies.

Frequently Asked Questions

Question 1   When should I design and pilot the data extraction form?

Data extraction can only take place after you have applied your inclusion criteria. However, a draft of your data extraction form can be designed very early in the review process. In fact, this may be done in parallel with writing your protocol. You can begin the process by looking at a key study that you have already identified for inclusion and thinking about the types of data you would extract from this study.

Question 2   How many studies should I use when piloting my data extraction form?

This will depend largely on the number of studies you have identified. For example, your searches may only have identified four or five studies, in which case you should pilot the data extraction form on two studies.

However, if you have 15 included studies, you might want to pilot your form on four or five studies.

Question 3   When is it too late to modify my data extraction form?

It is *never* too late to modify your data extraction form. If you discover, after completing your data extraction, that an important variable has not been extracted, then you can go back and extract these data from all of your studies. However, it is preferable not to find yourself in this situation as it can be time consuming to revisit individual studies (remember, you may also want somebody to cross-check all of your additional extraction).

Question 4   If data are recorded as raw numbers and I require percentages, should I calculate these values?

The short answer to this is yes. However, it may be sensible to have space on your form to record numbers and percentages, even if you do not describe both when writing up your review. Furthermore, it is sensible to make a note of where you have calculated numbers because they were not reported in the original studies. Be careful, you may make a mistake and therefore misrepresent the data and, remember, you may be challenged at some point about the origin of your numbers.

6

Understanding and Synthesizing My Numerical Data

Michaela Blundell

guide
supervisor studies outcomes
searches methods economics
protocol research
practical
meta-analysis quantitative systematic
synthesis student discussion databases management
FAQ post-graduate
question qualitative searching review
quality-assessment data
thesis

This chapter will help you to:

- present and interpret the numerical results of your included studies;
- recognize whether it is appropriate to combine your studies in a meta-analysis;
- understand the basic principles of meta-analysis;
- recognize heterogeneity and learn appropriate methods to deal with it;
- present and interpret the results of a meta-analysis.

Introduction

This chapter guides you through the processes of presenting and summarizing the numerical data presented in your included studies. We start by showing you how to present the results of individual studies and the best way to interpret them. We then explore the circumstances under which it is appropriate to combine data in a meta-analysis and explain what is involved in this process. We go on to consider the importance of heterogeneity and how you might deal with it in your analyses. We finish by suggesting how you can present the results of your meta-analysis and interpret your findings.

Points to note

Although this chapter has been written to guide you through the data synthesis process and explains the basic principles involved in a meta-analysis, it does not equip you with the skills to perform your own meta-analysis. Knowledge of the data-synthesis process will allow you to interpret study results correctly and knowledge of the principles of meta-analysis will help you decide whether using this technique is appropriate for your data. However, we always recommend that you talk to a statistician at key stages during the review process if you have not performed a meta-analysis before. A statistician will be able to check that your decision as to whether, or not, to perform a meta-analysis is sensible. S/he can advise you on the correct methods for performing a meta-analysis using the software you have available and can also help you to understand the results. You need to speak to your supervisor if you think you need advice from a statistician but don't know how to find one.

Before reading any further, it is important for you to know that a meta-analysis is not a required element of a systematic review. Meta-analysis should only be carried out as part of the review process if data from included studies are sufficiently similar and it is sensible to combine them. We looked at the titles and abstracts of 288 postgraduate theses included in the Dissertation and Theses database, dating from 1990 to 2012, which reported the use of systematic review methodology across a wide range of disciplines. We identified that a minority (n = 48, 17 per cent) of these contained a meta-analysis. There are a number of conditions that must be met before deciding to meta-analyze your data; if these are not fulfilled then it is inappropriate and misleading to combine data. Don't worry though; we'll talk you through this decision.

It is important to note that this chapter focuses solely on meta-analyzing evidence from randomized controlled trials (RCTs) because most of the current statistical methods use data from this type of study. Meta-analyses of observational data are becoming more common. For more information on the meta-analysis of non-randomized studies please refer to Chapter 13 of the Cochrane handbook (Higgins and Green, 2011).

Presenting and interpreting the results of individual studies

Chapter 5 focused mainly on using text to describe the data in your tables. It only briefly considered how you might describe the numerical data in your study results table. As numerical data can vary widely from study to study we are now going to look at this type of data more closely. The first thing to think about is the type of data that you are presenting. This chapter guides you through some of the most common types of data and the ways in which the data can be presented. It is not your job to manipulate the data as the authors of the published studies should have done this for you – use this chapter simply as a guide to help you to understand the information that is reported in the studies.

Binary data

Binary data are outcomes that can only be expressed as one of two possible responses, for example dead or alive, success or failure. These data may be presented by reporting: the number of patients who experience the outcome of interest in each treatment group and the number of patients randomized to each group (for example, on treatment A, 44 of the 60 patients experienced the event); the percentage of patients experiencing the event in each group and the number randomized to that group (for example, of the 60 patients on treatment A, 73 per cent experienced an event); summary statistic (relative risk, odds ratio or risk difference). The summary statistic is a point estimate which is the 'best guess' of the direction and size of the treatment effect. The direction of the treatment effect tells us which treatment is better and the size tells us by how much. An associated confidence interval is usually reported alongside the point estimate and is used to describe the uncertainty around the estimate by giving the range of values within which the true effect is strongly believed to lie. Confidence intervals can be reported for a number of significance levels; the most common is the 95 per cent confidence interval, which can be interpreted as meaning that the true effect lies within the range of the confidence interval 95 per cent of the time. A standard 95 per cent confidence interval can be calculated using the following equation:

95% confidence interval =

$$\text{summary statistic} \pm 1.96 \times \sqrt{\text{standard error of the summary statistic}}$$

Narrow confidence intervals indicate that the treatment estimate is relatively precise whereas wide confidence intervals suggest that there is a high degree of uncertainty.

Relative risk is the risk of an event in one treatment group divided by the risk in the other treatment group, where the risk is defined as the probability of the event occurring. If the two treatments being compared have the same effect, the relative risk is 1. If treatment A is better than treatment B, the relative risk of A relative to B is less than 1 and the relative risk of B relative to A is greater than 1. For example, if the relative risk of treatment A relative to treatment B is 0.67, this can be interpreted as meaning that the risk of an event on treatment A is 67 per cent of the risk of an event on treatment B. Put another way, there is a 33 per cent reduction in risk for patients on treatment A relative to those on treatment B.

Odds ratio is the odds of an event in one treatment group divided by the odds of an event in another treatment group, where odds are defined as the ratio of the probability of the event occurring relative to the probability of the event not occurring. This sounds a bit complicated but these odds are the same as those used in gambling to work out your financial gain if you win. For example, odds of 3:1 mean that for every £1 you bet, you win £3. Similarly, odds are often used in medicine, where a chance of survival of 50:50 means that for every 50 patients that survive, 50 die. In the same way as relative risk, if the two treatments being compared have the same effect, the odds ratio is 1. If treatment A is better than treatment B, the odds ratio of A relative to B is less than 1 and the odds ratio of B relative to A is greater than 1. Odds ratios are much less intuitive to interpret than relative risks. For example, an odds ratio of 0.54 indicates that there is a 46 per cent reduction in odds but this does not really tell us very much. To interpret what an odds ratio means in terms of the change in the number of events across treatment arms it is necessary to transform the odds ratio into a relative risk. People often incorrectly assume that relative risks and odds ratios are the same. When events are rare, the value of these two measures will be approximately equal, but as risks and odds increase large differences may exist between the two statistics.

The risk difference is the risk of an event in one group minus the risk in another group, where risk is defined as the probability of the event occurring (the same definition of risk as used to calculate a relative risk). This describes the absolute change so that if two treatments have the same effect, the risk difference is zero. If treatment A is better than treatment B, the risk difference of A relative to B is less than zero and the risk difference of B relative to A is greater than zero. For example, if the risk difference of treatment A relative to treatment B is −0.39, this indicates that the risk of an event is 39 per cent lower on treatment A than it is on treatment B.

How to calculate summary statistics for binary data if they are not presented in a published paper

Let's assume that Table 6.1 shows the trial outcomes reported in one of your included studies. The number of patients who experience the event (treated here as a failure) are denoted as F_A and F_B depending on whether they receive treatment A or B, and similarly patients who do not experience the event (treated here as a success) are denoted as S_A and S_B.

Table 6.1   Possible trial outcomes from an included study

Treatment	Event (Failure)	No event (Success)	Total
Treatment A	F_A	S_A	N_A
Treatment B	F_B	S_B	N_B

Relative risk

The relative risk is calculated by dividing the risk of an event on treatment A by the risk of an event on treatment B:

$$\text{relative risk} = \frac{F_A / N_A}{F_B / N_B}$$

An alternative way of presenting this information (provided that the treatment reduces the risk of event) is the relative risk reduction, which is calculated as follows: relative risk reduction $= 100 \times (1 - \text{relative risk})$

Odds ratio

The odds ratio is calculated by dividing the odds of an event on treatment A by the odds of an event on treatment B:

$$\text{odds ratio} = \frac{F_A / S_A}{F_B / S_B}$$

Risk difference

The risk difference is calculated by subtracting the risk of an event on treatment B from the risk of an event on treatment A:

$$\text{risk difference} = \frac{F_A}{N_A} - \frac{F_B}{N_B}$$

Table 6.2 shows outcome data from an RCT. The outcome is presented as the number (n) of patients experiencing an infection, the number of patients for whom there are data that can be analyzed (N) and the percentage of those patients who have data that can be analyzed and who experience an event (%). These numbers can be used to calculate relative risks, odds ratios and risk differences.

First, we need to rearrange the data in Table 6.2 into a 2 x 2 table, as shown in Table 6.3.

Table 6.2   Example of events reported in an included study

	Treatment arm			Control arm		
Trial	n	N	%	n	N	%
Smith 2012	2	32	6	3	40	8

Table 6.3   Example of trial outcomes reported in an included study

	Infection (Failure)	No infection (Success)	Total
Treatment arm	2	30	32
Control arm	3	37	40

$$\text{Relative risk } = \frac{2/32}{3/40} = 0.83$$

This can be interpreted as meaning that the risk of experiencing an infection in the treatment group is 83 per cent of the risk in the control group. Put another way, there is a 17 per cent ($100 \times [1 - 0.83]$) reduction in risk for patients in the treatment group relative to those patients in the control group.

$$\text{Odds ratio } = \frac{2/30}{3/37} = 0.82$$

This measure is much less intuitive to interpret than relative risk. An odds ratio of 0.82 means that there is an 18 per cent reduction in odds for patients in the treatment group relative to those patients in the control group but this doesn't tell us anything about the change in the number of events for patients in the treatment group compared with patients in the control group.

$$\text{Risk difference } = \frac{2}{32} - \frac{3}{40} = -0.0125$$

This can be interpreted as meaning that the risk of an infection is 1.25 per cent lower in the treatment group than it is in the control group, or that treatment reduces the risk of infection by 1.25 per cent.

Continuous data

Continuous data are outcomes measured on a continuous scale, for example age or height. These data may be presented separately for each treatment (for example, with a mean and standard deviation) or as a summary statistic that measures the difference between two treatments (for example, mean difference or standardized mean difference). If a summary statistic is not presented, we suggest you calculate this yourself as it is more meaningful than presenting the results separately for each treatment group.

The two measures described below assume that the outcomes you have extracted from your included studies have a normal distribution in each arm of each study. This means that the data tend to be distributed around a central point with no bias to the left or right. This assumption is not always met as data may be skewed; skewed data are not evenly distributed around a central point, rather they are clustered to either the left or right. Under such circumstances the mean is no longer the measure of choice. If you have concerns that your data may be skewed, speak to a statistician about the best approach to take.

Mean difference

Mean difference (this should really be called the difference in means) is the absolute difference between the mean values of the outcome in the two treatment groups. The mean difference is simple to interpret; a mean difference of 4.5 signifies that the outcome is 4.5 units bigger in one group than in the other.

Standardized mean difference

When studies assess the same outcome but measure it using different scales, the standardized mean difference (standardized difference in means) is used instead of the mean difference as it is necessary to standardize the results of the studies to a uniform scale. The standardized mean difference is a measure of the treatment effect that takes into account the variability observed across the participants. While standardized mean differences correct for different lengths of scales, they do not correct for differences in the direction of the scale.

The standardized mean difference is more difficult to interpret than the mean difference as it is reported in units of standard deviations rather than in the units originally used to measure the outcome. The Cochrane Handbook (Higgins and Green, 2011) discusses a 'rule of thumb' for interpreting this summary statistic as proposed by Cohen (1988): 0.2 represents a small effect, 0.5 a moderate effect and 0.8 a large effect.

How to calculate summary statistics for continuous data if they are not presented in a published paper

The mean difference is calculated simply by subtracting one mean value from the other:

Mean difference = experimental group mean − control group mean

The standardized mean difference is calculated using the following equation:

$$\text{Standardized mean difference} = \frac{\text{experimental group mean} - \text{control group mean}}{\text{pooled standard deviation}}$$

For information on calculating a pooled standard deviation please refer to Practical Statistics for Medical Research (Altman, 1991).

Example 1: Age

If you want to know the difference between two groups in terms of their mean age you would calculate the mean difference because the outcome is measured on the same scale in both groups (Table 6.4).

Table 6.4   Age of participants reported in a published paper

Group	Age of participants (years)										Mean age
A	56	62	57	55	59	57	58	55	54	58	57.1
B	58	61	64	62	63	61	59	63	60	62	61.3

Mean difference = 61.3 − 57.1 = 4.2 years

The mean difference indicates that on average, patients in group B are 4.2 years older than those in group A.

Example 2: Scores on tests

If you want to know the difference between two groups in terms of their test scores and group A's test was marked out of 60 and group B's test was marked out of 80 (as shown in Table 6.5), you couldn't use the mean difference as this wouldn't take into account the fact that the two tests were marked on different scales; instead, you would need to calculate the standardized mean difference as this adjusts for the difference between the two scales.

Table 6.5   Calculating mean differences in two groups' scores

Group	Score										Mean	SD*	Pooled SD*
A	46	52	59	55	49	43	54	57	60	56	53.1	5.59	
B	73	77	64	59	78	66	75	74	67	69	70.2	6.20	8.34

*SD = standard deviation

$$\text{Standardized mean difference} = \frac{70.2 - 53.1}{8.34} = 2.05$$

According to Cohen's rule of thumb, discussed earlier, there is a large effect (as the standardized mean difference is greater than 0.8). This means that there is evidence of a difference between the two groups after allowing for the fact that the two tests had different maximum scores.

Ordinal data

Ordinal data fall into ordered categories, for example, mild, moderate and severe. Methods for meta-analyzing ordinal outcome data are complicated and often unnecessary. It is common to analyze ordinal data with numerous categories as if the data were a continuous outcome; and ordinal data with few categories by grouping categories together and treating them as a binary outcome.

Count data

Count data are expressed as a total of the number of events that each participant experiences, for example, the number of infections patients experience during a clinical trial. Count data can be split into two types: counts of rare events and counts of common events.

For rare events, analyses of counts are based on rates that quantify the number of events occurring over a given time period. The summary statistic used for rare events is known as the rate ratio, which is calculated by dividing the rate of the event occurring in one treatment group by the rate of the event occurring in the other group. For example, if in treatment group A there are 14 events in a 24-hour period and in treatment group B there are three events in a 24-hour period the rate ratio is calculated by dividing 14 by 3, giving an answer of 4.7. This can be interpreted as meaning that the event of interest occurs 4.7 times more frequently in treatment group A than in treatment group B over a 24-hour time period.

For common events, the outcome can be thought of as the number of events in a treatment group and analyzed as if it were continuous data.

Time-to-event data

Time-to-event (survival) data are outcomes that measure the time taken for each participant to experience an event from a specified starting point. For those who do not experience the event of interest during the time they are observed, the length of time that they are in the trial is still recorded and they are classed as 'censored'.

It is possible to analyze time-to-event data in the same way as binary data by splitting patients into those who have experienced an event and those who have not experienced an event at a specific time period, but this requires knowledge of whether all patients have experienced the event or not at a given time point. The most common approach is to use survival analysis. This quantifies the data in terms of hazards, which are similar to risks (as mentioned in the binary data section) but are more unstable as they may change dramatically over time. Hazard ratios are interpreted in the same way as relative risks; a hazard ratio of 0.43 means that the risk of experiencing an event in one treatment group is 43 per cent of the risk of experiencing an event in another treatment group in a given time period.

Results tables

It is considered best practice to present the results of the included studies in a combined study results table. As discussed in Chapter 5, complementary text should describe any similarities and differences that you have identified across the trials rather than be focused on the results of individual trials. It is important that what you write in the text *exactly* matches what is shown in the table. Table 6.6 is a hypothetical results table showing the results of four lung cancer trials.

Table 6.6　Example results table (randomized controlled trial data)

Trial	Deaths			Infections		
	Arm A n (%)	Arm B n (%)	OR (95% CI)	Arm A n (%)	Arm B n (%)	OR (95% CI)
Jones (2012)	72 (29.9)	105 (43.2)	0.56 (−1.59 to 2.72)	NR	NR	NR
Price (2010)	152 (29.7)	244 (48.0)	0.46 (0.22 to 2.55)	312 (60.9)	448 (88.2)	0.21 (−1.92 to 2.33)
Smith (2012)	98 (32.6)	136 (45.9)	0.58 (−1.55 to 2.71)	206 (68.4)	241 (80.9)	0.51 (−1.58 to 2.74)
Wadsworth (2013)	62 (27.4)	94 (40.9)	0.55 (−1.62 to 2.72)	144 (63.7)	201 (87.4)	0.25 (−1.96 to 2.46)

OR = odds ratio; CI = confidence interval; NR = not reported

The following is an example of the text that might go alongside Table 6.6:

> Four trials report outcomes in this patient population. Number of deaths was reported in all four trials, but only three papers reported number of infections. Across the trials, death rates ranged from 27.4 per cent to 48.0 per cent and infection rates ranged from 60.9 per cent to 88.2 per cent.

Meta-analysis

First things first: what is a meta-analysis and why might you want to do one? A meta-analysis is a statistical technique that allows results from individual studies to be combined to give an overall measure of the effect of one treatment compared with another (Glass, 1976). Meta-analysis allows the results from several trials to be combined; such analyses (usually) include a large number of patients, and therefore may have more power to detect smaller (but still clinically significant) differences than an analysis of results from a single trial. This means that meta-analyses can be particularly useful when analyzing subgroups; for example, if there are too few patients in the subgroups of individual trials to allow any differences to be detected. In addition to being able to detect smaller differences, any estimates detected by a meta-analysis will be more precise (that is, narrower confidence intervals) because as the number of patients increases the variability between patients is reduced.

The main assumption underlying a meta-analysis is that the trials are sufficiently similar for the results to be combined, that is, they are homogeneous. However, it is inevitable that trials will differ in some way or another. The important thing is that you should be confident that they are not too heterogeneous to be grouped together and that it is sensible to combine the results to get an overall measure of effect. The following sections outline the key steps involved in understanding if and how you might perform a meta-analysis (see Table 6.7).

Table 6.7   Key steps to consider when synthesizing data using meta-analysis

Step 1	Assess whether it is appropriate to combine your studies in a meta-analysis
Step 2	Justify your decision to conduct (or not) a meta-analysis in your text
Step 3	Choose an appropriate meta-analysis method
Step 4	Identify and discuss any heterogeneity in the meta-analysis results
Step 5	Present and interpret the results of your meta-analysis

Step 1 Assess whether it is appropriate to combine your studies in a meta-analysis

Once you have presented the results of your included trials, the next task is to decide whether it is appropriate to combine the results of the studies in a meta-analysis. It is appropriate to combine study data in a meta-analysis only if the assumption of homogeneity is satisfied. Before being able to satisfy the assumption of homogeneity, four aspects need to be assessed. The first is that trials should be similar in terms of the patients they recruit. This can be checked by examining inclusion criteria and patient characteristics across trials. This is a subjective approach as there is no quantitative measure of patient similarity.

The second aspect for consideration is that the trials should be comparing the same interventions (or exposures) and comparators; trial publications should provide detailed descriptions of each. It is important to check that these are consistent across the trials as, if they differ substantially, you will not be comparing like with like. For example, if you are looking at drug trials, it is important to check for details of treatment doses, duration of treatment and any supplementary care given alongside the investigational treatments.

The third aspect is that trials should be reporting the same outcomes. It may be that the primary outcomes for each trial differ, but that there are common secondary outcomes across trials. Not only should the outcomes reported be the same, but the time frame over which they are measured should also be comparable. If the outcome of interest happens gradually over time and some trials are only measuring the outcome for 24 hours while others are looking at the outcome over 7 days, the event rate in the shorter trials will be different from the event rate in the longer trials.

The fourth aspect is that the results of the trials should show that the treatment effects are generally in the same direction (that is, all showing that one treatment is better than another, or all indicating that there is no difference between treatments) and the corresponding confidence intervals overlap. A good way to check this is by producing a forest plot using a statistical software package. The square in the center of each line shows the point estimate of the treatment effect recorded in each study and the line shows the corresponding confidence interval. The size of the square is proportional to the size of the study, so larger studies will have a larger square. The length of the line is proportional to the width of the confidence interval, so longer lines indicate wider confidence intervals and therefore less accurate treatment effect estimates. The diamond at the bottom of the plot shows the overall estimate of the treatment effect and corresponding confidence interval. The center of the diamond indicates the point estimate of the treatment effect and the width of the diamond

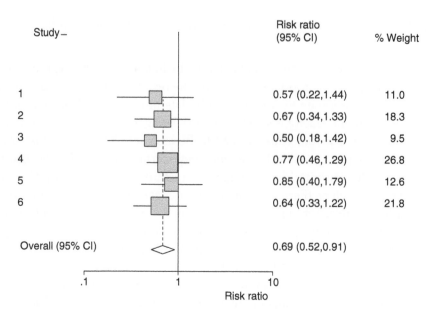

Figure 6.1   Example of a forest plot showing it would be appropriate to perform a meta-analysis

represents the width of the confidence interval. When the individual study estimates of treatment effect are relatively consistent and have confidence intervals that overlap (Figure 6.1), it is appropriate to pool results in a meta-analysis.

When estimates vary widely and confidence intervals do not overlap (Figure 6.2), this suggests that the trials are too dissimilar and that it may be inappropriate to pool the results in a meta-analysis.

It is important to ensure that you enter the trial results into the statistical software program in a consistent manner; results are presented comparing one treatment to another so it is important to make sure that in each case the same treatment is used as the reference treatment. If trial data are entered inconsistently, it might look like the trials' results differ greatly, when in actual fact they are similar.

If your data satisfy all four criteria then you are ready to perform a meta-analysis and obtain an overall measure of treatment effect. However, before we move on, let's think about what to do if your data don't satisfy all of the criteria.

If only some of your included trials meet all of the criteria then it may be sensible to perform a meta-analysis only on those trials that meet these criteria. If this is the case, then you should also carry out a sensitivity analysis by adding the remaining studies to test the robustness of the

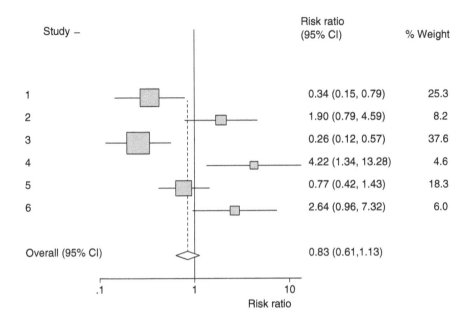

Figure 6.2   Example of a forest plot showing it would not be appropriate to perform a meta-analysis

results. Similarly, if all of your included trials meet the majority of the criteria, then it may still be sensible to combine them in a meta-analysis. In both cases you must make it clear in your report that all criteria were not met by all of the included trials and you must fully explain the implications that this may have on your results. If all of your trials do not fulfil any of the criteria (and this is highly probable) then performing a meta-analysis would be inappropriate. Combining your data would not be sensible as the overall measure of the treatment effect would be misleading. Under these circumstances the data should be synthesized narratively.

Step 2   Justify your decision to conduct (or not) a meta-analysis in your text

Whether you decide to perform a meta-analysis or not, it is important that you can justify your decision in the text of your thesis. As previously mentioned, if your data satisfy all four criteria then you are ready to perform a meta-analysis and obtain an overall measure of treatment effect. However, a meta-analysis is not a required element of a systematic review and it is advisable to clearly set out the reasons why you did not perform one.

So, what might you write to explain why you have not performed a meta-analysis and how might you describe what you have done instead? The following text provides an example:

> A meta-analysis was not performed. Only a narrative summary of the data is presented. The differences across the trials, including poor quality of the trial reports, diversity of protocols, and the inconsistency in reporting of outcomes, precluded a statistical synthesis of the included trial results.

Step 3   Choose an appropriate meta-analysis method

The first mistake people make when carrying out a meta-analysis is to simply pool all of the data from the separate studies as if they were all from one study. If you do this, you fail to preserve the randomization employed in each of the individual trials and you introduce bias and confounding (these concepts are addressed in Chapter 4). When trials are being designed, investigators put considerable effort into ensuring that the two (or more) treatment groups are similar in terms of the patients who are enrolled. By 'lumping' patients from different trials together, you may no longer be comparing like with like; it is therefore important to maintain randomization when combining data from your included studies.

Another common mistake is to simply calculate an arithmetic mean of the treatment effects of the different studies. This approach is inappropriate as it gives all studies equal influence over the size of the overall treatment effect. The results of small studies are generally deemed to be less accurate than results from larger ones, the confidence intervals around the results are usually wider so results are less precise and smaller studies are also more likely to detect a treatment difference when it does not actually exist. For these reasons, smaller studies should be given less weight in a meta-analysis. A meta-analysis needs to include a weighted average of the treatment effects whereby the results from larger trials take precedence over the results from smaller ones.

A meta-analysis can be performed in two steps. The first is to identify or calculate a summary statistic (relative risk, odds ratio or risk difference for binary data; differences in means for continuous data) for each study. The second step is to calculate the weighted average for this statistic. There are various techniques for calculating the weighted average depending on the summary statistic that is being analyzed and the choice of weighting method. The techniques available all take a similar approach and are all derived from the following formula:

$$\text{Weighted average} = \frac{\text{Sum of (estimate} \times \text{weight of individual study)}}{\text{Sum of weights}}$$

There are a number of different methods available for performing a meta-analysis (see Table 6.8 for some of these) and they can be classified into two main models – 'fixed effects' and 'random effects'. The fixed effects model assumes that there is one true effect observed across all studies and that any variability between the studies is due simply to chance. In comparison, the random effects model assumes that the true effect varies from study to study but that it is centered on some overall average treatment effect.

Table 6.8   Different approaches to meta-analysis

Outcome measure	Fixed effects analysis	Random effects analysis
Binary		
Relative risk	Mantel–Haenszel, Inverse variance	DerSimonian Laird
Risk difference	Mantel–Haenszel, Inverse variance	DerSimonian Laird
Odds ratio	Mantel–Haenszel, Inverse variance, Peto	DerSimonian Laird
Continuous		
Mean difference	Inverse variance	Inverse variance
Standardized mean difference	Inverse variance	Inverse variance
Count		
Rate ratio	Inverse variance	Inverse variance
Survival		
Hazard ratio	Inverse variance	Inverse variance

Meta-analysis can be performed using one of a number of computer software packages; a comprehensive list of these and how to use them is discussed in the book *Systematic Reviews in Health Care: Meta-analysis in Context* (Egger, Smith and Altman, 2001). One of the most popular software packages for this is RevMan, the Cochrane Collaboration's software for preparing and maintaining Cochrane reviews, which is freely available. Another widely used statistical software package is STATA. You will be able to perform a meta-analysis using STATA but, unlike RevMan, you will not be able to complete all aspects of your systematic review within it. STATA is not free to download but it may be available through your academic institution.

Step 4   Identify and discuss any heterogeneity in the meta-analysis results

Meta-analyses rely on the fact that the trials included in them are sufficiently similar to allow them to be combined. However, we know that it is inevitable that the trials differ in some way or another. In meta-analysis, heterogeneity is a measure of the variability between studies. It can be split into three types: clinical heterogeneity, which is the variability in participants, interventions and outcomes; methodological heterogeneity, which is the variability in trial design and quality; and statistical heterogeneity, which is the variability between the study results that is more than would be expected due to chance alone.

You need to examine the forest plot to identify whether there is substantial heterogeneity. If the studies are estimating the same thing, we would expect their confidence intervals to overlap; if there is poor overlap this indicates that heterogeneity is present. This 'eyeballing' approach is very subjective and is simply used to give you an initial overview. Next you would use the chi-squared test for heterogeneity to carry out a more formal assessment of heterogeneity. This test allows you to assess whether the observed differences in treatment effects are due to chance alone; a low p-value indicates that heterogeneity is present. This test should be used with caution when there are only a few studies, or when the number of patients recruited to each study is small, as in such cases it is unlikely to detect heterogeneity even if a moderate amount is present. For this reason, a p-value of 0.1 is often used for determining significance, rather than the typical level of 0.05. It should also be noted that a non-significant result cannot be taken as evidence of homogeneity. The use of the chi-squared test is also problematic when there are a large number of trials; under these circumstances the test may detect clinically unimportant levels of heterogeneity.

After establishing that heterogeneity is present, you may want to calculate the degree of heterogeneity. This can be measured using the I^2 statistic. The I^2 statistic describes the percentage of the total variation across studies due to heterogeneity rather than chance and results lie between 0 and 100 per cent. A value of 0 per cent would indicate that no heterogeneity was observed and as the value increases the level of heterogeneity increases. As a rough guide, 25 per cent represents low heterogeneity, 50 per cent represents moderate heterogeneity and 75 per cent represents high heterogeneity.

If you identify a large amount of heterogeneity, one way to deal with it is simply to acknowledge the problem and *not* report the results of the meta-analysis. It is important to ensure that you make it clear to the reader that you think it is inappropriate to combine the results as they vary considerably and that you consider that combining them would invalidate the overall estimate of the treatment effect.

Alternatively, you may still decide to report your results but include a caveat to let the reader know that you have concerns about the reliability of your results. We do not recommend using a fixed effects meta-analysis when there is a large amount of heterogeneity as this invalidates the main assumption of the fixed effects analysis, that is, that there is one underlying true effect measured across all trials. A random effects analysis takes account of any unexplained heterogeneity between your studies but it does not explain the reasons for heterogeneity. For this reason, a full investigation of heterogeneity is still required.

Subgroups and sensitivity analysis

Heterogeneity is commonly investigated using subgroup analysis. Subgroup analyses determine whether different treatment effects are observed in different subgroups of patients. For example, a larger treatment effect may be observed in younger patients compared with the effect observed in older patients. If this is true, and there are wide differences in the ages of patients in different trials, then this could be one reason for heterogeneity. If trials present data on subgroups, you may want to meta-analyse the data for each of the subgroups to see how the overall treatment effect compares across the different subgroups. Examples of how to carry out subgroup analysis within a systematic review can be found on our website (www.liv.ac.uk/systematic-review-guide).

Another, more advanced, way to investigate heterogeneity is to use a statistical technique known as meta-regression. This technique adjusts the meta-analysis to take into account factors that are thought to influence the treatment effect (such as age) (Cooper, 2010). Alternatively, you may wish to perform sensitivity analyses, including and excluding certain trials from the analysis to test the robustness of the results.

You should think in advance about any factors that are to be considered when exploring heterogeneity and specify these in your review protocol. If factors are identified after heterogeneity has been detected your results may be criticized because you are looking for reasons without an a priori rationale.

Step 5   Present and interpret the results of your meta-analysis

The best way to present the results of a meta-analysis is by using a forest plot and you can produce these easily using RevMan software (Higgins and Green, 2011). A forest plot presents the individual results of all studies as well as the overall combined estimate of the treatment effect. It is important to label each of the individual results. It is also useful to present the individual study results numerically along with the weights that have been assigned to each study.

As well as presenting the results visually in a forest plot, you need to provide complementary text which summarizes and discusses the results. The results of the overall treatment effect can be interpreted in much the same way as if they were from an individual study. That is, if the meta-analysis combined binary data then the overall treatment effect would be presented as an odds ratio, risk difference or relative risk; if continuous data were combined, then the effect would be presented as a mean difference or standardized mean difference; if survival data were combined then a hazard ratio would be presented. The case study at the end of this chapter includes further details on presenting and interpreting the results of a forest plot.

Final thoughts

This chapter has focused on combining the numerical results of RCTs in a meta-analysis. Remember, this step isn't a prerequisite for a systematic review of quantitative data. If your review includes non-randomized data and you are thinking about performing a meta-analysis, then you really should speak to a statistician and/or your supervisor as there is currently no gold standard approach for synthesizing the results of this type of research.

Key points to think about when writing your protocol

- Whether you intend to perform a meta-analysis and how you will decide if it is appropriate to do so;
- What kind of outcome data you are likely to find;
- What type of summary statistic you will use in your meta-analysis (if appropriate);
- How you will identify and deal with heterogeneity in your meta-analysis (if appropriate);
- Whether you will perform any subgroup analyses or meta-regression and what factors you might adjust for in these analyses (if appropriate).

What an examiner is looking for in your thesis

- Clear interpretation of the results from your included trials;
- Full description of whether your included studies meet the criteria for conducting a meta-analysis;
- Rationale for undertaking or not undertaking a meta-analysis;
- Valid approach used to perform a meta-analysis (if meta-analysis was undertaken);
- Appropriate assessment of heterogeneity (if meta-analysis was undertaken).

CASE STUDY

How to present and interpret a forest plot

The plot in Figure 6.3 shows an advantage for treatment A over treatment B; the point estimates are all to the left of the vertical axis indicating that all studies favored treatment A over treatment B, and the diamond representing the pooled effect is also to the left of the axis. This advantage can also be seen in the risk ratios reported on the right, which are all less than 1. The pooled result reinforces this (risk ratio = 0.69) and the 95 per cent confidence interval suggests a statistically significant advantage for treatment A over treatment B as it doesn't contain 1 (95 per cent confidence interval = 0.52 to 0.91). The relative risk of 0.69 means

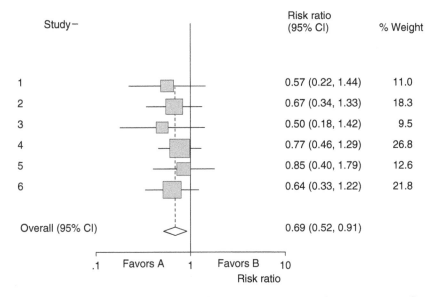

Study		Risk ratio (95% CI)	% Weight
1		0.57 (0.22, 1.44)	11.0
2		0.67 (0.34, 1.33)	18.3
3		0.50 (0.18, 1.42)	9.5
4		0.77 (0.46, 1.29)	26.8
5		0.85 (0.40, 1.79)	12.6
6		0.64 (0.33, 1.22)	21.8
Overall (95% CI)		0.69 (0.52, 0.91)	

.1   Favors A   1   Favors B   10
Risk ratio

Figure 6.3   A forest plot showing an advantage for treatment A over treatment B

(Continued)

(Continued)

that patients' risk of experiencing an event is reduced by 31 per cent (1 to 0.69) whilst on treatment A relative to the risk whilst on treatment B. The 95 per cent confidence intervals all overlap, suggesting that the degree of heterogeneity is small, but this should be assessed more formally by using a chi-squared test.

Frequently Asked Questions

Question 1 **What if my included studies measure the same outcome but not at the same time point?**

If your studies measure the same outcome but at different time points, you might want to contact the authors of the studies to ask for more information on a common time point and then use these data in a meta-analysis. If it is not possible to get data on one time point for all studies, then it would not be appropriate to combine the data in a meta-analysis; you should only combine the data that are measured at the same time point.

Question 2 **What if the outcomes are defined differently across the studies (for example, different definitions of common primary study outcome)?**

If outcomes are defined differently across studies, it is advisable to perform sensitivity analyses whereby studies that define outcomes differently are removed and/or replaced to test the robustness of the overall results.

Question 3 **What if the studies I have included in my meta-analysis are of varying quality?**

If the studies vary greatly in quality it is sensible to perform a sensitivity analysis. A sensitivity analysis involves, for example, excluding lower-quality results and re-running the meta-analysis. This will test the robustness of the overall results of your original meta-analysis.

Question 4   What if I only found one trial?   2 or more ✗

If you have only identified one suitable trial for inclusion in the review then it will not be possible to synthesize your data in a meta-analysis; instead you should simply narratively describe the results of the single trial.

Question 5   If I have only two included trials, is it worth carrying out a meta-analysis?

Two trials is the minimum number of trials required before you can perform a meta-analysis. However, the accuracy of the meta-analysis results increases with the number of included studies. So, if you only identify two trials that are appropriate for inclusion, you can still perform a meta-analysis but you will need to explain the limitations of including only two trials when you write up your thesis.

7

Writing My Discussion and Conclusions

M. Gemma Cherry

guide
supervisor studies outcomes
searches methods economics
protocol research
practical
meta-analysis quantitative systematic
synthesis discussion databases management
student
FAQ post-graduate review
question qualitative searching
quality-assessment data
thesis

This chapter will help you to:

- understand the importance of the 'Discussion' and 'Conclusions' sections of your thesis;
- gain an awareness of what to include in these sections, and why;
- recognize common pitfalls and learn how to avoid them.

Introduction

Well done! You are coming to the end of the systematic review process. In this chapter we provide advice on how to write the final sections of your systematic review – your 'Discussion' and 'Conclusions' sections. We start by outlining the purpose of these two sections and why they are important. We go on to talk you through the general principles involved. To help you through the process, we then discuss common pitfalls and how to avoid them.

What are the 'Discussion' and 'Conclusions' sections and why are they important?

The purpose of these sections is to provide a critical interpretation of the results of your review in relation to the review question that you set out to answer. No matter how meticulously you conduct your review, if the discussion and conclusions do not reflect the nature and limitations of the research process and the evidence you have presented, then you have not appropriately addressed your research question. The discussion and conclusions are essential parts of your thesis and of any subsequent publications arising from it.

Mullins and Kiley (2002) wrote an informative paper looking at *how* examiners examine a thesis by surveying 30 experienced thesis examiners. Whilst individual styles varied, the general consensus between examiners was that they begin by reading the abstract, introduction and conclusions to gauge the scope of the work and they then read the whole thesis in detail. When reading a thesis they tend to ask themselves things like: 'How would I have tackled the problem set out in the title and abstract?' and 'Do the conclusions follow on from the introduction?' In any document, the 'Conclusions' section represents the culmination of a lot of work. It is, therefore, important to remember that the examiner will often turn to this section first. If this section seems rushed then it is likely to influence how an examiner perceives the rest of your thesis, so it's important to invest time into making sure that your conclusions are as good as they can be.

It is our experience that students spend the vast majority of their time carrying out the early activities of the review, including data extraction and data synthesis and analysis, and that very few students take adequate time to reflect on the possible interpretations of the data and the conclusions that can be drawn. It's important to leave sufficient time to think through the results of your review and their importance, particularly in terms of discussing your results in the context of your review question. Similarly, if you're planning to publish your review in a journal, it's worth bearing in mind that readers often skim read the majority of the paper and turn to the discussion and conclusions of a review to find the review's 'take home messages'. As a student, academic and systematic reviewer, you have a responsibility to the readers to ensure that your discussion of findings and your conclusions are accurate, evidence-based, appropriate and applicable to your review question.

How do I write my discussion and conclusions?

Your discussion and conclusions need to be clearly structured and make logical sense to the examiner. We recommend including the points set out in Box 7.1 although the exact order in which you discuss each point may vary depending on your review question.

Box 7.1

Main components of the discussion and conclusions

1. Did I find all of the evidence that I thought I would?
2. Was I able to answer my review question?
3. How do my findings fit with previously published research?
4. What are the strengths and limitations of the included studies?

---

5. What are the strengths and limitations of the review process?
6. Can the findings be generalized?
7. What conclusions can be drawn from the review?
8. What are the implications of the review for professional practice and/or future research?

Did I find all of the evidence that I thought I would?

The first section should discuss your search strategy and its appropriateness. Did you find an abundance of literature or was there very little? Was this because of what was available, or because the search strategy was inappropriate? If you found a great deal of literature you may have decided to limit your research question – this is where you discuss that decision and the implications that you consider it had on the review. You finish this part of the discussion with a conclusion about whether you believe you have all, or at least a representative sample, of the available evidence relating to your question. This gives the reader your view on whether the appropriate literature has been identified for consideration.

Example:

Application of the inclusion criteria to the results of the searches identified 15 empirical papers for inclusion in this review, a surprisingly small number given the recent growth in editorials and review pieces advocating the application of attachment theory to the study of patient–doctor communication. Nonetheless, piloting of the search strategy and supplementation of the results of the electronic search with hand searching and searching of reference lists of included papers allows confidence in the conclusion that all relevant research was included in this systematic review and that conclusions arising from this review can be based on synthesis of all available evidence. (Cherry, 2013)

Was I able to answer my review question?

This should be a simple statement summarizing the main finding of your review. If there isn't sufficient evidence from which to draw a conclusion then you need to make this clear in your text. There is no need to repeat the 'Results' section here – the purpose is to remind the reader of the overall key findings so that they have a reference point when reading the rest of your discussion.

Example:

> All studies assessing the efficacy of oral flecainide and propafenone reported
> favorable results in comparison to other treatment strategies. Oral sotalol was not
> found to be as efficacious as intravenous digoxin-quinidine. (Saborido et al., 2010)

How do my findings fit with previously published research?

Consider outlining how your findings fit with the research that you outlined
in the 'Introduction' section of your thesis. Do your findings contradict common practice or national policy? Do the data you have support existing
theory? Are you surprised by your findings?

Example:

> Although there may be other reported life benefits to its use, we found no con-
> vincing evidence that consistently demonstrates the effectiveness of any particular
> biofeedback treatment in the control of hypertension when compared with
> pharmacotherapy, placebo, no intervention or other behavioral therapies. This
> is in line with previous literature demonstrating little to no effectiveness of any
> particular biofeedback treatment in this clinical population.

What are the strengths and limitations of the included studies?

Systematic reviews are designed to combine available data, so *there should be
very limited discussion of individual studies*. The majority of the discussion needs
to focus on what the research tells you when you consider the data overall. If
the quality of your included studies is good then you will have more confidence in the results of your studies and the conclusions of your review. How
consistent are the findings across different studies? How similar are the participants or outcome measures used? This is your chance to summarize your
view on the extent to which data from the included studies allowed you to
answer your review question.

Example:

> Overall, the methodological quality of the included trials was poor. All stated
> that patients were randomly allocated to treatment groups; however only four
> studies described the method of randomization and only two of these noted

how allocation was concealed. The majority of trials included either no post-treatment follow up or less than 6 months' follow up. There were 15 studies with post-treatment periods of 6 months up to a maximum of 12 months. (Greenhalgh et al., 2009)

What are the strengths and limitations of the review process?

It is important to discuss the strengths and limitations of the review process itself. Was your search strategy comprehensive? Did you include non-English papers, or theses? Did you assess the quality of your included studies (the answer to this should be yes and this is a strength of your review)? Did anyone (a peer, or your supervisor) cross-check your extracted data? Did you perform appropriate analyses? Did you consider publication bias? You may also include a discussion of the appropriateness of your inclusion criteria in this section. It may be that because of your broad inclusion criteria you ended up with a number of studies that actually did not address the question you were asking, or that the participants were so different across studies that you ended up 'comparing apples with oranges'. If you invested time in the development of your research question then this should not happen, but sometimes it does. In the discussion you can explain why this has happened and reflect on how this may have influenced your review findings. In these circumstances it is important to discuss fully any papers containing data directly related to your review question.

This section of the discussion gives you the opportunity to outline the limitations of your review. If you can correctly identify the limitations then this will help you to interpret your findings in the appropriate context, thus demonstrating insight and reflection on your part. It is important to remember that this section is a platform that can be used to highlight the strengths of the research and make it clear to the examiner that you understand the review process and your findings. If you have followed the steps outlined in this book then you will have produced a high-quality systematic review. Make sure that you demonstrate that your review is clear, thorough, reproducible and transparent.

Can the findings be generalized?

This question can be answered by drawing together what has been explored in the previous sections. You need to focus this part of your discussion on the implications of the review and its generalizability to your research question and professional practice. To whom do the results apply? Should caution be used when translating the results to certain populations? It's important to consider the quality of included studies and the review process when writing this section.

Example:

> The trials were disparate in terms of their design, patient populations, interventions and definition/reporting of outcomes (clinical and safety) which means it is difficult to compare outcomes across the trials or perform evidence synthesis with any confidence using only the summary data reported in the published studies. (Greenhalgh et al., 2011)

What conclusions can be drawn from the review?

The end of the 'Discussion' section should provide *your* view of the answer to *your* review question based on the data *you* have presented. There is no consensus on how much detail should be in the 'Conclusions' section. Reviews of effectiveness papers tend to have very short 'Conclusions' sections; the conclusions tend to be, 'Yes, the treatment works and we should be using it', 'No, it does not work and we should not be using it' or 'We don't know if it works because there isn't sufficient (high-quality) research'. Social science researchers often use the 'Conclusions' section to explore the options relating to future action that is required as a result of the findings of the review. In contrast, the results of qualitative reviews often explore the richness and context of the data that have been reviewed. There is no right or wrong way and we suggest that you take the lead from your supervisor in following departmental or institutional preference.

Example:

> Uncertainty in the available clinical data means there is insufficient evidence to support a recommendation for the use of the pill in the pocket strategy in patients with paroxysmal atrial fibrillation. (Saborido et al., 2010)

What are the implications of the review?

Every systematic review has implications, be they clinical, educational, research or policy related. First, the implications of your review should be discussed in terms of the relevant client groups. For example, in health care reviews of effectiveness, implications are generally considered in terms of patient care or public health, and for educational reviews, the implications for students or teachers are generally discussed.

Second, this section should also include a discussion of the need (if any) for future research. Avoid saying, 'More research is needed' and try to focus on the study that you would like to see take place. Give clear direction about study design, choice of outcome measure, participant groups etc. It often helps to base these implications on the findings of your quality assessment exercise by identifying where included studies were found to be lacking.

There is currently a vibrant debate regarding the role of systematic reviews in making recommendations for policy. The emerging consensus is that the findings of one systematic review are not sufficient to allow policy-makers to draw firm conclusions; the results of several systematic reviews may need to be considered by experts, who may also take into account risk, cost and patient preference before making policy decisions.

Example:

> Future research should consider and address the methodological and conceptual limitations of currently published findings. It should aim to assess the relationship between attachment style and objective, behavioral outcomes, transferable to the clinical setting, with the goal of establishing a theoretical, observable link between attachment style and communication. Such research should be adequately powered and should consider incorporating a longitudinal study design to ensure the most rigorous and conclusive findings. (Cherry, 2013)

Common pitfalls and how to avoid them

From our collective experience of supervising students, we can tell you that one of the most frustrating things for a supervisor is to read an excellent thesis which falls apart towards the end because the student didn't take sufficient time to fully consider their findings and write their discussion and conclusions. Box 7.2 summarizes some of the most common reasons that students write poor discussion and poor conclusions.

Box 7.2

Common reasons for poor discussion and conclusions

The students:

- didn't answer or address the review question;
- didn't leave sufficient time at the end of the project to adequately examine and consider their data;
- didn't have enough confidence in themselves and their experience to draw firm conclusions from the data – too scared of 'getting it wrong';
- had too much confidence in themselves and made grand, sweeping, over-generalized statements;
- had data that did not match the results they were hoping to get;
- didn't understand their data or their analysis and so couldn't adequately conclude anything from their review;
- didn't critically appraise their work or its implications.

Not answering the review question: The most important aspect of the 'Discussion' and 'Conclusions' sections is that you actually address your review question (see Chapter 2). This may sound obvious, but it is surprising how many students fail to answer their review question. This most frequently happens when students don't clearly define their review question, or don't have a clear protocol to follow. The students who have made these mistakes often end up wandering their way through the evidence and are still wandering whilst writing their discussion because they didn't have a clear idea of their final destination, or they found something else that they thought was more interesting or important and ignored their original question.

Too little time: It is important to work back from your submission date and set a research timetable to ensure that you meet your target deadlines (see Chapter 10). Unlike other research projects where you're encouraged to meet timelines because of external commitments to others, when you're undertaking a systematic review as a student, you're working primarily independently and therefore self-discipline is required. Sometimes the best laid plans go awry due to unforeseen circumstances – you had to wait longer than you had planned for papers from the library, or your dog ate your hard drive midway through your write up. What's important is that you don't take that lost time from the time you've allocated to the write up, especially the write up of the discussion and conclusions. You'd be surprised how frequently this happens, particularly when the student isn't sure of their data or how to discuss them.

When writing up it is also not uncommon for students to gloss over the findings of their quality assessment exercise. This is an error and one which is likely to be picked up by an examiner – see Chapter 4 for hints on how the quality of included studies can impact on the conclusions of a review.

Results need to be mulled over or considered during a walk in the park. This will not happen if you are writing up your discussion at midnight the night before your thesis is due to be submitted. It is easy to spot these kinds of reports – we have frequently seen well-conducted systematic reviews that have been carried out meticulously with almost nothing written in the discussion and conclusions because the student spent all of their time and energy on the description of what they did and far too little time writing up what it all meant.

Unsure of yourself and your opinions: If you chose a topic of genuine interest to you then this is less likely to be an issue than if your topic area was unfamiliar to you, or worse, bored you from the very beginning. You've probably spent months reading around, and summarizing, the research in a topic area that you already care about and are likely to already hold, or at least want to develop, an opinion about this specific issue or topic. So be confident enough to say what you think. Others can disagree with your opinion, but a well-formulated examination and report of the data that have been presented is what is expected of you at this level (see Chapter 5 and Chapter 6). What your examiner wants to see is evidence of the thought processes and critical thinking that brought you to your conclusions about the data. Your examiner wants you to show that you have explored the implications of your data and wants to see how you think current practice, or your approach to your professional work, will benefit from the review that you have carried out. The examiner of your thesis might not always agree with your conclusions, but if you have presented a clear case as to why you came to those conclusions then you have succeeded in your work.

Too much confidence: Be careful not to be too confident, or sweeping, in your discussion or conclusions; both need to be firmly grounded in the context and limitations of the included data and also the review process. If you didn't include theses or gray literature then say so – but don't then conclude that you've summarized all of the available evidence and go on to draw conclusions with 100 per cent certainty. Every review and study has its limitations; it's important to recognize them and not to include broad statements without references or supporting data to back them up.

The data do not say what you want them to say: This happens far more frequently than most people would like to admit. If you are carrying out a review in a topic area that interests you then you probably already have an opinion about it. All too often, these opinions are not upheld by the research findings that you summarize. This can be a good finding and can provide you with a starting point for your discussion; it's often very interesting to read discussions that say that 'Current practice in the area is X but the research says Y' and to read the reviewer's take on the reason(s) for this finding. What you must not do, however, is try to adapt your data to match your views. It can be frustrating to have mentally written your discussion before properly interpreting the data only to find that you have to reformulate your arguments. It is far better to take the time to re-think your ideas during the review process, rather than be challenged by an examiner or peer reviewer at a later date.

You do not understand your data: This is a real problem and usually happens when you don't leave sufficient time to explore your findings (see Chapters 4 and 5). It also often occurs when statistical analysis has been carried out and you're unfamiliar with the analysis and/or what the results really mean (see Chapter 6). Equally, this can be a problem when all of your included studies use different outcome measures, or research participants come from very diverse settings. It's important to understand what your data mean before you attempt to discuss them or draw conclusions. This might mean spending a bit more time considering your data, chatting to a statistician or your supervisor, doing some wider reading, or simply taking a break from your review for a few days. Whatever you do, it's important to fully understand the implications of your findings. If the study outcome measures or participants are too diverse to statistically synthesize, then say so. If you can't draw conclusions from the data due to the presence of heterogeneity, then that's OK. You can recommend that future research focuses on a more homogeneous set of participants or outcomes.

Lack of critical appraisal: The examiner marking your thesis will be checking whether you have demonstrated your ability to critically examine the evidence and that you understand what the data mean. This is something that the majority of students struggle with – they can describe the data that they have extracted but the majority fail to provide their reflection on what the data actually mean. Critical appraisal is important because it shows that you understand the data and the limitations of the research. It's not sufficient to assess the quality of studies and report the findings in a table in the 'Results' section but not refer to the table again. Good and well thought out critical appraisal is what separates exceptional students from average students and demonstrates a reviewer's ability to not only discuss findings but to understand their meaning in terms of their clinical, educational or policy implications.

It can be frustrating for an examiner to read a thesis where the student follows all of the steps but doesn't think about what the findings mean; if one study reports a strong treatment effect for drug A but only tests it on two people, then you need to develop the skills to interpret these findings in relation to the study that found no effect on 1,000 people. A discussion should never be a list of 'Smith said, Jones said and Walley said'. It needs to examine and discuss the included studies as a group, highlighting where there are similarities and differences. Then you need to discuss what you think are the possible reasons for these similarities and differences. This is what critical appraisal means and it is a vital part of every systematic review. Critical appraisal skills can be difficult to develop but there are a number of excellent books and online educational materials to help you. Further information can be found on our website (www.liv.ac.uk/systematic-review-guide).

Final thoughts

You're now coming to the end of the six specific chapters focusing on the practical elements involved in the systematic review process. Throughout this book, the systematic review process has been likened to a journey. As with any journey, unless you know the route well, you would expect to consult your map numerous times along the way, particularly if you get lost. Treat this book, in particular Chapters 2 to 7, like your map. Turn down page corners, highlight text and scribble notes to yourself in margins. Re-visit chapters that discuss concepts or methods that you are unsure about and skip through chapters discussing those aspects that you are most confident about. Most importantly, make sure that you keep this book with you throughout the review process as it can act as a handy guide, particularly when you feel lost.

The next two chapters are for students who have specific journeys in mind: qualitative reviews and reviews of cost-effectiveness evidence. By all means read them, even if you don't plan to carry out these types of reviews, but be aware that whilst they touch on points already discussed in previous chapters, they are designed to be very topic-specific. However, don't forget that the final chapter in the book (Chapter 10) contains useful advice on planning and managing your review, irrespective of the type of review you conduct.

> ## Key point to think about when writing your protocol
>
> • Most protocols don't require sections on discussion and conclusions because when you write your protocol you usually have no idea what you will find.

> ## What an examiner is looking for in your thesis
>
> • Sensible discussion of study results based on intelligent interpretation of the data;
> • Orderly discussion of important points – keep discussion of similar points together;
> • Reflection on your methodological and analytical choices and explanation of how these choices may have influenced your conclusions;
> • Conclusions that come from critical consideration and are supported by evidence from included studies.

Frequently Asked Questions

Question 1   What if I don't have any studies to discuss?

It would be unusual to carry out a systematic review as part of a Master's degree with no included studies, particularly given that a large proportion of the marks for your review will come from your ability to quality assess the included studies and extract and synthesize relevant data from them. If, however, you choose to progress with no studies then your 'Discussion' section is likely to be the most important part of your review, with a lengthy explanation of the reasons why you didn't find any studies and the research implications arising from your review. It would be important, in such a case, to explain that you carried out the review because you felt that there should be studies conducted in the topic area. The fact that you didn't find any studies implies either that the topic area should be highlighted as a research priority or that it isn't generally considered to be important. We recommend that you explore both interpretations. Be sure to include a discussion of the strengths and limitations of your review process too; even though you didn't find any studies, there will be adequate room to discuss your methodological approach and its pros and cons.

Question 2   What if I disagree with the findings?

It can be frustrating when you have a mental picture of what you think you will find, but then the data suggest something entirely different. In this case it is important to have an open mind and try to interpret your findings with respect to the data. If you expected to find an effect but didn't, you might want to think about why you expected to find that result. Are there methodological considerations in the included papers that may have influenced the findings? For example, did the papers consider only participants aged over 65, whereas you based your hypothesis on participants aged 18–65? In cases such as this, it is often valuable to discuss your findings with your supervisor or a peer; often students can't see the forest for the trees and getting other perspectives really helps to reframe and reinterpret unexpected data.

Question 3   What if I discover that the way I have been doing things is wrong?

At this point, it is probably too late to re-do your review. The best that you can do is make sure that you reflect on what went wrong, why it went wrong, and how this may have influenced your findings. It might be something out of your control, such as you couldn't access any papers from a certain journal. It might be that you missed out a key search term, or your review question was far too broad. As long as you reflect on the potential implications of your (perceived) errors on the conclusions and the implications arising from your review, you are demonstrating awareness and reflection. It happens to the best of us, so don't beat yourself up too much. Discuss your concerns with your supervisor and try to account for what has happened when writing your 'Discussion' and 'Conclusions' sections.

8

Reviewing Qualitative Evidence

M. Gemma Cherry, Elizabeth Perkins, Rumona Dickson and Angela Boland

guide
searches methods supervisor studies outcomes
protocol research economics
meta-analysis quantitative practical systematic
synthesis discussion databases management
FAQ student post-graduate
question qualitative searching review
quality-assessment data
thesis

This chapter will help you to:

- understand the principles of qualitative evidence synthesis and how these differ from quantitative evidence synthesis;
- define a qualitative review question;
- be aware of the possible approaches to synthesizing qualitative research;
- understand issues specific to qualitative evidence synthesis.

Introduction

We are assuming that, since you are reading this chapter, you are thinking about conducting a systematic review of qualitative evidence. In this chapter we re-visit the principles outlined in previous chapters but place emphasis on reviewing qualitative evidence. In particular, we outline why we think qualitative evidence synthesis is important, how the steps you take can differ from those involved in quantitative evidence synthesis, and finally we outline some of the challenges, rewards and pitfalls associated with qualitative evidence synthesis.

Why should I carry out a review of qualitative evidence?

Qualitative data synthesis aims to bring together the findings from qualitative literature to allow consistencies or differences in findings to be identified (Tong, Flemming, McInnes, Oliver and Craig, 2012). It also allows gaps to be found or meta-level themes and/or conclusions to be developed. Whilst quantitative evidence synthesis generally allows determination of whether something works (or not), qualitative evidence synthesis allows such issues to be explored in more depth, for example by considering what works for whom, and why. It allows for synthesis of the perspectives of participants and can provide rich data relating to the impact of a condition, intervention, or policy on the lived experiences and feelings of those involved. Bringing together the findings from qualitative research can lead to a greater understanding of the sensitive issues that such research frequently addresses. Qualitative evidence synthesis provides an excellent opportunity for students to learn, and then apply, the principles of systematic reviewing. If your topic area of interest lends itself to qualitative evidence synthesis then we encourage you to go ahead. It will be an excellent learning experience for you as a student and also as a researcher.

Differences between qualitative and quantitative evidence synthesis

Reviews of quantitative evidence generally follow a series of distinct steps which are outlined in Chapters 2 to 7. These steps are clear and well tested, and form the basis of a 'gold standard' systematic review of quantitative evidence. However, these steps leave little room for interpretation, particularly in reviews of clinical effectiveness where the conclusions often take the form of 'A is better at treating X than B, but isn't as good as C'.

Whilst researchers carrying out qualitative reviews follow a series of defined steps, these steps are less prescriptive than those involved in reviews of quantitative evidence, particularly with respect to quality assessment, analysis and synthesis of data. The good news is that in reviews of qualitative evidence, you have freedom to decide on how best to analyze your data. On the flip side, this means you have to defend your chosen analysis technique and make it very clear in your write up why you chose one method over another. Whilst five researchers performing the same quantitative meta-analysis should come up with exactly the same conclusions, five researchers applying the same review question to qualitative data may end up with five completely different sets of conclusions, depending on each researcher's choice of analysis, synthesis method and theoretical standpoint.

Reviews of qualitative evidence may provide richer conclusions than reviews of quantitative data due to the potentially greater depth of analysis. There are fewer right and wrong answers with qualitative research; but be warned, this type of synthesis requires the researcher to be reflective and flexible in their approach.

Do I follow the same steps as in a quantitative review?

If you're thinking, 'Hang on, I've just trawled through the whole book and now you're telling me the principles differ between reviews of qualitative and quantitative evidence!', then don't worry, you haven't wasted your time. There are a number of common key steps involved in conducting a systematic review, be it quantitative or qualitative, which we have outlined in great detail in Chapters 2 to 7. The key differences lie in data extraction, quality assessment and synthesis. However, if you have just picked up this book and flipped to this chapter without reading the previous chapters then *stop*! Pour yourself a drink and read the book from the beginning. You'll understand a lot more about what's covered in this chapter if you already have an idea of the general principles of systematic reviewing. The main principles of systematic reviewing qualitative evidence map onto those of reviewing quantitative evidence, and are outlined in Table 8.1.

Table 8.1   Main principles of qualitative and quantitative evidence synthesis

Step	Review of qualitative evidence	Review of quantitative evidence
1	Review question, scoping searches and protocol	
2	Literature searching	
3	Screening titles and abstracts	
4	Obtaining papers	
5	Selecting full-text papers	
6	**Theoretical standpoint and analysis plan**	**Quality assessment**
7	**Data extraction and quality assessment**	**Data extraction**
8	**Analysis and synthesis (Qualitative)**	**Analysis and synthesis (Quantitative)**
9	Writing up and editing	

As you can see from Table 8.1, like a quantitative review, there are nine key stages to a systematic review of qualitative evidence. Most of these steps will be exactly the same regardless of whether you're reviewing qualitative or quantitative data. However, some will require additional considerations, and so we'll discuss each step from a qualitative review perspective, highlighting where the steps differ from those involved in reviewing quantitative evidence.

Nine key steps in a qualitative review

Step 1   Identifying your review question, carrying out scoping searches and writing your protocol

Chapter 2 discussed the importance of establishing a clear research question, and laid out a number of steps for you to follow. The main additional points that you need to consider when reviewing qualitative evidence are:

1 Is my review question clear and applicable to the available qualitative data?
2 Have I developed a set of inclusion criteria applicable to qualitative evidence synthesis?

It may well be that you begin your research with what you believe is a clear question. For instance, you may want to know mothers' views on treating fever in their infant children. Or you may want to understand the experience of mothers who have to return to work and need to place their infants in nurseries. These may seem like quite straightforward questions but very few qualitative research studies will have asked exactly these questions. Indeed it is more likely that studies have addressed these questions within broader studies, such as those relating to basic care issues or the role of day-care nurseries. This is where scoping searches relating to child care would prove useful. They will allow you to have a look at the current state of the literature and evaluate the suitability of your question. Alternatively, as you carry out your scoping searches you may identify that there are other, more important, issues within each of these topics, and you may decide that you want to modify your question and follow where the research leads. This is a very acceptable qualitative approach but, be aware, it can often take up a great deal of time.

The second task that differs somewhat from the steps involved in quantitative evidence synthesis is the development of your inclusion criteria. Whilst quantitative reviews generally define inclusion criteria in terms of PICO or 'who, what, how and where' tables, the inclusion criteria used in qualitative reviews tend to be less specific. Rather than trying to devise a PICO table, we recommend that you think of your inclusion criteria in terms of PICo: **p**opulation, phenomena of **i**nterest (which may be either a condition or an intervention) and the **co**ntext (Joanna Briggs Institute, 2011).

Conceptualizing the components of a review idea, or topic area, in terms of PICo helps you to plan what kind of studies you intend to include in your review without being so specific that you risk excluding a potentially relevant paper. This approach also provides the examiner, or other readers, with a significant amount of information about the focus, scope and applicability of your review in relation to their needs. Table 8.2 provides two examples of PICo tables for qualitative evidence synthesis.

Table 8.2   Example PICo tables

Review question	What are the views of mothers regarding treatment of fever in their infant children?	What experiences do mothers returning to work and placing their infants in nurseries report?
P	Mothers with infant children	Mothers with new infants
I	Views around treatment of fever in infants	Coping with emotional responses
Co	Home	Day-care nurseries and home

We recommend that you follow the principles laid out in Chapter 2, modifying your inclusion criteria accordingly, and being aware that the time it takes to develop a qualitative review question is often longer than the time it takes to develop a quantitative review question. Setting out your plans in a protocol is a great way to organize your thoughts. Amend your timelines accordingly, and begin this process with patience and curiosity.

Step 2   Literature searches

Chapter 3 talked you through searching for evidence. The general principles are the same when searching specifically for qualitative studies. However, you need to think carefully about how you are going to find studies that have addressed your specific research question within broader qualitative studies. A specific, detailed and complex search strategy may not be as helpful here as in a quantitative review given that some papers have relevant data that may be hidden in the depths of a larger study. Rather than try to put together a complicated search, it might be better to consider combining a number of free text words relating to your PICo table, using AND, OR and NOT. Using a broader and less precise search strategy will yield more titles and abstracts to examine during screening. This, in turn, means that you will have to look at more full-text papers than if you were conducting a quantitative review with very narrow and tightly defined parameters. However, this broader approach allows you to identify 'fuzzy' papers that you might not otherwise have found. It's also worth searching a variety of databases. MEDLINE is not necessarily the preferred choice for qualitative research. We recommend that you start by searching CINAHL as this database has indexed qualitative studies more completely and for longer than other databases (Flemming and Briggs, 2007). Be aware that sometimes qualitative researchers can be quite creative with their titles and so you might wish to spend time before you start searching familiarizing yourself with key index terms and subject headings that are relevant to your review question.

We recommend that, in addition to terms reflecting your topic, you add generic terms (like 'qualitative' or 'findings') to the terms listed below; reviewers at ScHARR organize these under the abbreviation ESCAPADE (see Table 8.3). Also, don't forget to supplement your enquiries with searches of reference lists, hand searching and also searches using Internet search engines. This stage, as with all searches, will be trial and error, but it is worth investing time to ensure that your searches have the appropriate balance of sensitivity and specificity (as mentioned in Chapter 2).

This is a good time to raise the question of how many studies you need to include in a qualitative review. It is an important question and one frequently posed by students conducting systematic reviews. If you draw upon methods from primary qualitative research then you will search only until

Table 8.3   ESCAPADE

E	Exploratory methods: Include search terms related to the methodology of interest, such as focus group, grounded theory, action research
S	Software: Include search terms related to software researchers may have used to analyze their data, such as NVivo or Nudist
C	Citations: Include key references, both in your specific research area and more globally in the qualitative research arena
A	Application: Consider searching terms related to the wider application of potentially relevant studies, such as ethnology or psychology
P	Phenomenon: Include search terms related to the phenomenon of interest, such as perceptions, attitudes, view points, standpoints
A	Approaches: Consider searching for different methodological approaches, such as ethnography
D	Data: Think how researchers may have 'labelled' their data in their paper and include terms such as stories, narratives, themes
E	Experiences: Similarly, consider how researchers may have conceptualized participants' experiences, using terms such as encounters

Note: We have permission to reproduce this table from Andrew Booth at ScHARR you have retrieved sufficient studies to demonstrate that any additional studies do not provide any new information – you have, in qualitative terms, reached saturation (Box 8.1). The standard systematic review approach, however, is to include all studies that meet your inclusion criteria and therefore you carry on searching and applying inclusion criteria to all identified research papers. Neither approach can be considered the 'right way'. What is important is that you decide on your approach, describe it clearly and, in the limitations section of your thesis, point out how your decision might have impacted on the conduct of the research and, very importantly, on your findings and your conclusions. It is worth thinking about how you might deal with this issue before your start your review. Discuss your plans with your supervisor and consider including a section in your protocol on how many studies you will search for and/or include in your final review.

| Box 8.1

Evidence saturation

A Master's student, Saul, decided to carry out a systematic review to identify how online learning programs are being evaluated in terms of student learning. He couldn't decide whether to synthesize qualitative or quantitative evidence, and was leaning towards quantitative evidence until he carried out his scoping searches and realized that the majority of published literature available was qualitative in nature (an interesting finding in itself). Saul began his review but realized quite early on in the process that the evaluation reports from relevant online learning programs were very similar in terms of their objectives, outcomes and results. He discussed this with his supervisor and decided to stop searching for more studies as finding more studies reporting the same data would not add anything to his qualitative review.

Step 3 Screening titles and abstracts

As we said earlier, if you use a broad and inclusive search strategy, then you will have lots of studies to sift through at this stage. Remember, using your inclusion criteria to identify studies for possible inclusion in the review can take up a lot of your time so factor this into your plans. Also, be aware that, compared with a quantitative review it is likely to be more difficult to spot potentially relevant papers at this stage. Be inclusive rather than exclusive to maximize your chances of obtaining relevant full-text papers.

Step 4   Obtaining papers

If you're going to be inclusive when screening titles and abstracts, then it is likely that you will be obtaining more papers than your peers who are carrying out quantitative reviews. Don't worry. There isn't a limit on the number of full-text papers that you can obtain. Just make sure that you have sufficient budget (for example, if you have to pay for inter-library loans) and that you have allowed sufficient time to carry out this stage of your review.

Step 5   Selecting full-text papers

It follows that if you are obtaining more studies then you will have more studies to select from than your peers who are carrying out quantitative reviews. Take your time. Read each study carefully to identify all relevant data and, using your inclusion criteria, make a decision about its applicability to your review. Again, factor in an appropriate amount of time for this stage so that you don't panic when you find that you have lots of full-text papers to screen.

Step 6   Determining your theoretical standpoint and analysis plan

Now you've got a final list of your included studies it's important to consider your theoretical standpoint and your analysis plan. This needs to be done before you start quality assessing studies, extracting data or producing tables. Qualitative researchers can adopt many different approaches, such as grounded theory, ethnography and thematic framework analysis to name but a few; however, unlike quantitative research there is no hierarchy of evidence among methodologies for qualitative studies. So you can't say one study is 'better' than another because it uses a 'better' methodology.

It is argued that the synthesis of qualitative data needs to be based on a defined philosophical backdrop. Ring and colleagues provide a detailed discussion of the relevant literature (Ring, Ritchie, Mandava and Jepson, 2011). In qualitative research, the tradition of the methodology is embedded within all aspects of the research process. For example, discourse analysis is an approach that runs through data collection, analysis and write up. Therefore, the findings have to be assessed in relation to the fidelity of the method. Basically, you have to choose how you want to analyze your data before you start, because it will influence the data you extract, how you look at your data and how you draw conclusions from them.

There are many ways to analyze qualitative data. If you quickly search the Internet using the term 'qualitative evidence synthesis' you'll find the terms qualitative meta-synthesis, qualitative meta-narrative, qualitative meta-ethnography, grounded meta-analysis, meta-summary, qualitative meta-aggregation and qualitative evidence synthesis used in different settings with different definitions and, at times, used interchangeably. Each refers to a slightly different approach. We appreciate that, in contrast to quantitative data synthesis, the world of qualitative synthesis can appear to be very complex and confusing. The main thing to remember is that, unlike quantitative meta-analysis, the aim of a qualitative systematic review is to broaden the reader's understanding of a certain phenomenon through the consideration of themes within, or across, qualitative data. We won't go into too much more detail on the different approaches available as there are a number of excellent books and sources for each method of qualitative synthesis (Centre for Reviews and Dissemination, 2009; Joanna Briggs Institute, 2011). We recommend that you consult Table 8.4 and Figure 8.1 and read up on your chosen approach *before* you attempt to carry out any form of data extraction or synthesis.

It is important to keep in mind that there is no single correct approach. You need to make a decision based on what suits you, your research question and your approach to the review. However, whatever approach you use, you need to ensure that you provide the reader with a clear overview of the method you have chosen and your reasons for choosing it. Don't make your analysis decision for the wrong reasons. Examples of incorrect reasons for choosing an analysis method are displayed in Box 8.2.

Table 8.4 Methods of qualitative synthesis

Term	Definition
Meta-narrative	A means of identifying 'storylines' across different qualitative research. Traditionally used to inform policy making.
Meta-ethnography	A means of drawing together studies with the goal of producing new meaning or theoretical understanding. This is currently the most widely adopted method of data synthesis.
Meta-aggregation	A means of assembling the conclusions of primary studies (however reported) and pooling them on the basis of similarity in meaning.
Meta-summary	A means of 'mapping' the contents of qualitative research studies.
Grounded meta-analysis	Analysis grounding the content of the text within the context where it was constructed.
Qualitative evidence synthesis	Reviews that synthesize and analyze findings from empirical qualitative research.

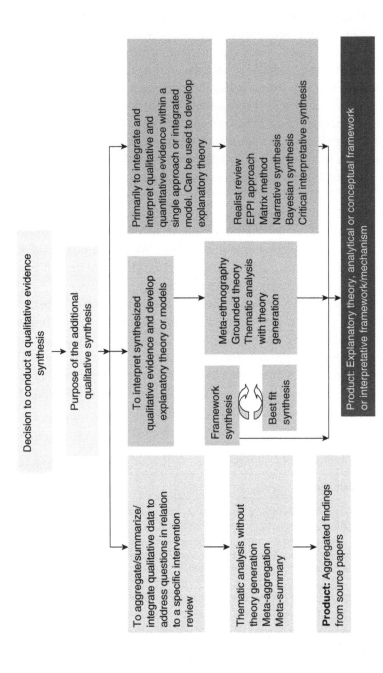

Figure 8.1 Methods of choosing qualitative synthesis technique

Note: We have permission to reproduce this figure, adapted from published guidance from the Cochrane Collaboration Qualitative Methods Group (Noyes and Lewin, 2011), from Andrew Booth at ScHARR

Box 8.2

Incorrect reasons for choosing an analysis method

Lucy chose her analysis technique because all of the systematic reviews she had read used meta-ethnography. She deduced that all these 'proper' researchers couldn't be wrong.

Penny spoke to Amy, who had previously used meta-aggregation in a review. Amy managed to carry out her review with few problems and passed her Master's degree, so Penny concluded that meta-aggregation would be an appropriate approach.

Rahul chose realist synthesis because he had been to a conference and it was the one everyone was talking about.

Anna was going to use meta-summary but spent the afternoon talking it through with Fabio, who had had a bad experience using meta-summary. She changed her mind and went with framework synthesis because it seemed straightforward.

Jan wasn't sure, so she spoke to her supervisor, Noah. Noah told her to use meta-narrative, so she did.

Why are these reasons wrong? None of the students considered their review question and/or data when they made decisions about their preferred methods of analysis and synthesis. Their decisions may well have been correct, but not one of them spent time considering the different methods available. They did not make their choices by thinking about what best fitted their data or the aims of their review.

Step 7 Data extraction, table production and quality assessment

Data extraction also differs between reviews of qualitative and quantitative data and, as with a quantitative review, can be approached in several different ways. You must always keep your review question in mind as you extract data, and always think, 'Are these data relevant to my review question?' We often print and laminate our review questions and put them in a prominent place by our computers so that they always catch our eye whilst we work on our reviews. Believe us, it helps.

As in any review, it is important to identify and put the key descriptive information from each study into tables. Some extracted data will be the same regardless of review focus, such as location and setting of study, but extraction of qualitative data will differ depending on your approach to synthesis. For example, you may wish to develop a framework and extract data relating only to specific themes. You may wish to interpret, and reflect on the data to create new themes. You may wish to report data from individual studies separately, or report meta-level themes. You may wish to reduce the findings into a small number of categories or into one finding. The nature of your data extraction depends on your analytical approach. As the type, and presentation, of data can differ a lot between synthesis approaches, we won't go into any further detail here (for more information see our website: www. liv.ac.uk/systematic-review-guide).

Take a look at other systematic reviews that have analyzed qualitative data using your choice of analysis method and explore how other authors have presented their data. There isn't a right or wrong way, but your data extraction needs to be tailored to your analysis approach, theoretical standpoint and the aim of your review. So spend time deciding how to proceed. It's OK to change your mind half-way through if you feel the data lend themselves to a different approach, but you must ensure that you provide the reader with a clear overview of the studies that you have included, their similarities and differences and your view of their findings. However how you choose to present these data is, to some extent, up to you.

You might decide to assess the quality of your studies prior to data extraction and exclude 'low-quality' studies, or you may choose to include all studies but report details of their quality as a narrative. Again, this depends on your synthesis approach; deductive (theory-testing) and inductive (theory-generating) analyses may differ in their inclusivity. We'll discuss quality assessment next but don't be afraid to undertake this task before extracting data.

There are many ways to assess the quality of qualitative evidence as part of a qualitative review. Flexibility is required when carrying out quality assessment as the included studies will almost certainly be based on different qualitative research approaches; there isn't a hierarchy of evidence like there is with quantitative study designs. Both the Centre for Reviews and Dissemination report (2009) and the report by Ring et al. (2011) provide excellent overviews of the quality assessment options for qualitative studies.

There are some basic quality assessment considerations that you may want to apply to qualitative studies. These include:

- Was the research guided by a clear question?
- Was the research conducted in an ethical and rigorous manner?
- Was there clear information about the methods that were used to collect and analyze the data?
- Did the research provide information that indicates the bias of the researcher(s)?
- Did the research provide information regarding whether the findings have been verified?

Additionally, when quality assessing qualitative research it is important to consider a number of issues that are not relevant when quality assessing quantitative research. These include the congruity between the stated philosophical perspective and the research methods, whether the theoretical standpoint of the researcher was considered and/or addressed, whether participants' voices were adequately represented and whether there was a statement as to the theoretical or cultural location of the researcher. As there is no accepted gold standard quality assessment tool, then what is important is that you clearly present the assessment that you carried out, why you chose that particular approach and what impact your approach had on the findings of your review.

Step 8 Analysis of qualitative data

We suggest that you take a look at the further reading section at the end of this book and visit our website (www.liv.ac.uk/systematic-review-guide), choose an appropriate text relating to your approach to analysis and synthesis and spend some time familiarizing yourself with the requirements or recommendations associated with that approach. You need to know how you will manage your extracted data before you begin the review process – your preferred methods should be explicitly stated in your protocol. Currently, new approaches to synthesis are regularly being developed by qualitative researchers. Qualitative tools such as NVivo have been used. The Joanna Briggs Institute has developed a software package called Qualitative Assessment and Review Instrument (QARI) for meta-aggregation. You will have to pay to use this package so check with your supervisor as s/he might already have access to it. Space does not allow us to provide extensive detail relating to the various approaches to synthesis that you might consider, but take a look on the Internet and read around this topic to help you get started.

Step 9 Writing up and editing

Quantitative systematic review write ups generally focus on the transparency of the review process and the explicit methods that have been followed, with emphasis placed on minimization of bias. Qualitative systematic review write ups follow the same principles. Keep your target audience (in your case, your examiner) in mind and be explicit about your theoretical standpoint and the limitations of your review process in your write up. Qualitative evidence synthesis gives you great freedom in your approach to analysis and synthesis, but it also means that when you write up your research you have to be very clear about why you made your decisions, and how your decisions have impacted on your conclusions. The write up is your chance to show that you have thought through your review from start to finish.

Key points to bear in mind during the review process

It's worth bearing in mind that there is currently an ongoing debate relating to the appropriateness of conducting systematic reviews of qualitative research. Some researchers see the drawing of conclusions from qualitative data at a population level, rather than at the level of individual research studies, as a difficult, if not impossible, task. This is because of the subjective nature of the individual experiences captured by qualitative research.

Each qualitative research project is different, and each researcher brings their own perspectives and theoretical standpoint to the analysis. Interpretation and reporting of data are therefore subjective; it's not as easy as saying 'Ten people died because they had drug X'. Because qualitative research starts with a view that phenomena are created and shaped within the social and historical context in which they are experienced, it becomes quite tricky to make comparisons with phenomena located in a very different time and context. In addition, a successful synthesis of findings relies on the reviewers' ability to identify the ideological, philosophical and methodological similarities between studies to allow the findings to be compared in a robust way; basically, you sometimes have to read between the lines and interpret what researchers haven't said as well as what they have said. Bear this in mind when you are carrying out your review.

Qualitative research is carried out for the purposes of illumination and interpretation. Qualitative research synthesis, therefore, allows reviewers to construct greater meaning from the results of primary studies. Such synthesis is needed to allow for the translation of findings into policy and so we advocate qualitative evidence synthesis and applaud you for choosing this path for your Master's thesis. Methods for synthesizing data from qualitative research are evolving and make the process both challenging and rewarding. In terms of your thesis, it can provide you with an opportunity to explore a variety of research approaches and gain a new perspective on the conduct of qualitative research and its use in practice.

Key points to think about when writing your protocol

- Clarity in your review question;
- Acknowledgment that a variety of qualitative research approaches might mean that synthesis of evidence is difficult.

What an examiner is looking for in your thesis

- Critical in-depth analysis of your findings;
- Critical appraisal of the review process and data analysis approach adopted;
- Reflection on your methodological and analytical choices and explanation of how they may have influenced your conclusions;
- Where appropriate, provision of alternative conclusions from the available data.

Frequently Asked Questions

Question 1 Can I combine qualitative and quantitative evidence within a single systematic review?

Yes, and these types of reviews are sometimes called integrative reviews. However, it's important not to underestimate how challenging these reviews can be to carry out. Few studies deal with topics in the same way and as a result it is often difficult to provide concrete conclusions about a particular topic using this type of approach. First, you need to be clear why you are doing the review and specify the research question that you are attempting to address. Second, you need to set out what prompted you to combine the two types of data – was it to gain as comprehensive an understanding of a particular topic as possible or was it to generate new insights into a particular phenomenon? Sandelowski et al. (2007) make a distinction between assimilation where the findings are incorporated into each other, and configuration, where the findings are used to generate new, or modify existing, theoretical or narrative accounts. Other authors use terms like aggregation and integration to reflect the different types of activity associated with systematically reviewing qualitative and quantitative studies. The approach most often adopted when undertaking a systematic review that combines qualitative and quantitative studies is to undertake separate systematic reviews of the 'evidence', assessing each body of research using methodologically, theoretically and disciplinary appropriate criteria, and then to bring them together once each synthesis has been completed.

Question 2 Can I undertake a systematic review of qualitative studies on any topic?

In short, yes. As long as research has been undertaken you can conduct a systematic review.

Question 3 Can I only review qualitative studies that adopt the same methodological approach?

No. Currently those involved in qualitative evidence synthesis are split into those who believe that only studies drawing upon the same research tradition should be combined and those with a more pragmatic view who consider that any type of qualitative evidence can be brought to bear in the quest to answer a particular question. You should decide where you place yourself in this debate and be prepared to justify your stance.

9

Systematically Reviewing Economic Evaluations

Angela Boland,
Sophie Beale and
M. Gemma Cherry

guide
searches methods supervisor studies outcomes
protocolresearch economics
meta-analysis quantitative systematic
synthesis discussion databases management
FAQ student post-graduate
question qualitative searching review
quality-assessment data
thesis

This chapter will help you to:

- develop your economic systematic review question;
- search for economic evidence;
- critically appraise economic evidence;
- draw conclusions from economic data.

Introduction

This chapter is written specifically to guide you when undertaking a systematic review of economic evaluations. First, we outline the purpose of a systematic review of economic studies. Second, we describe the types of economic studies you are likely to identify when searching for economic evidence. We also guide you through the key steps you are likely to undertake when reviewing economic evidence, highlighting where these steps differ from other types of systematic review.

Points to note

We feel that we must make several points clear about this chapter. Economic reviews are important but most students are not equipped to conduct them unless economics is their main area of study. We encourage these students to read on.

This chapter focuses on economic evaluations of health care interventions, our area of expertise. However, we are confident that the universal principles described in this chapter will also be useful if you are reviewing economic evaluations from any other field of study.

The main purpose of this chapter is to help you to complete your systematic review of economic evaluations on time and without too many problems along the way. We've assumed that you have studied, are studying, or at least understand the basic principles of economic evaluation. If you are interested in learning how to carry out an economic evaluation or how to build an economic model then, sorry, you will need to look elsewhere for information and you might find it helpful to consult the Health Economics textbooks and journal articles recommended on our website (www.liv.ac.uk/systematic-review-guide).

Reviews of economic evaluations fall into two types – reviews *of* economic evaluations and reviews *for* economic evaluations (Anderson, 2010). This chapter is written to help you complete a review *of* economic evaluations. The most frequently asked question in reviews of economic evaluations in the field of health care is, 'For a specific group of people, is intervention X cost effective when compared with intervention Y?' This chapter has been written with this question in mind.

Undertaking a review of economic evaluations is similar to undertaking a quantitative review. This chapter can be read as a stand-alone chapter, but you will find it more useful if you have already read Chapters 2 to 7. Each of these chapters contains information that will improve the content and quality of your thesis. In this chapter we offer you *additional* information that is specific to a review of economic evaluations.

What is a systematic review of economic evaluations?

A systematic review of economic evaluations is similar to any kind of systematic review of quantitative or qualitative evidence, in that it aims to bring together all of the available relevant evidence to answer a specific question. As with other types of review, a systematic review of economic evaluations might be designed to answer a specific question to inform decision making; it might be conducted to summarize methodological arguments with a view to reaching consensus; or it might be carried out to search for data to inform an economic model or an economic evaluation. Some reasons for carrying out economic reviews are shown in Table 9.1.

What type of studies might I find in a review of economic evaluations?

There are many types of economic evidence and these include economic evaluations, economic reviews, cost analyses, commentaries, editorials and letters. You can find economic evidence explicitly stated in the title or abstract of economic studies or lurking in the depths of a wide range of

Table 9.1   Reasons for carrying out a review of economic evaluations in health care

Why might you carry out a review of economic evaluations in health care?	Example
To find out which of two drugs offers value for money for a specific group of patients.	Is pemetrexed cost effective compared with gemcitabine for patients with non-squamous non-small cell lung cancer?
To identify the different types of economic models used in economic evaluations within a specific topic area.	What is the best way to model the costs of cardiac care in patients with multi-vessel disease?
To identify the available quality of life evidence for a specific group of patients so that you can then use this information in your own economic evaluation.	What is the best source of quality-adjusted life year values for patients with breast cancer in the UK?

publication types. For the purposes of this chapter, we focus primarily on economic evaluations and there are four main types: cost-minimization analysis (CMA), cost-effectiveness analysis (CEA), cost–utility analysis (CUA) and cost–benefit analysis (CBA). These four types are usually grouped together and called 'full' economic evaluations as they consider both the costs and benefits of health care interventions or programs. 'Partial economic' evaluations either do not involve a comparison between alternatives or do not relate costs to benefits; this type of study includes burden of illness/cost of illness studies (BOI/COI), cost-consequence analyses (CCA) or simply cost analyses.

In general, economic evaluations describe the costs *and* benefits of alternative courses of action, usually comparing innovative interventions with interventions that are gold standard or best practice. As shown in Table 9.2, the four types of full economic evaluation identify, measure and value the costs of interventions and comparators in the same way; they only differ in the way they identify, measure and value the benefits arising from the interventions and comparators. In health care, the most commonly used methods of economic evaluation are CEA and CUA. Both of these approaches use incremental cost-effectiveness ratios (ICERs) to summarize their results. For example, CEAs often report results in terms of incremental cost per life year gained (cost per LYG) and CUAs often report results in terms of incremental cost per quality-adjusted life year gained (cost per QALY).

Table 9.2   Types of economic evaluation studies

Full economic evaluations	Characteristics
Cost-minimization analysis (CMA)	Benefits are proven to be equivalent. Focus is on costs. Costs are measured in currency (for example, £ or $).
Cost-effectiveness analysis (CEA)	Benefits are uni-dimensional and measured in natural units (for example, cost per LYG). Costs are measured in currency (for example, £ or $).
Cost–utility analysis (CUA)	Benefits are multi-dimensional (for example, quality and quantity of life) and typically measured in QALYs. Costs are measured in currency (for example, £ or $).
Cost–benefit analysis (CBA)	Both benefits and costs are measured in currency (for example, £ or $).
Partial economic evaluations	**Characteristics**
Burden of illness (BOI)/cost of illness studies (COI)	Economic burden of a disease is measured and the maximum amount of money that could potentially be saved, or gained, if a disease or condition no longer existed is estimated.
Cost-consequence analysis (CCA)	Different costs and benefits of the interventions being compared are not aggregated. Benefits are measured in natural units (for example, number of people cured) and costs are measured in currency (for example, £ or $).
Cost analysis	No mention of outcomes; focus is solely on costs.

QALY= quality-adjusted life year; LYG=life year gained

What are the key terms used in economic evaluations of health care interventions?

Some of the key terms used in economic evaluations of health care interventions and programs are listed in Table 9.3. If you are planning to undertake a systematic review of economic evaluations then you need to be, at the very least, familiar with these terms as you won't be able to carry out your review successfully if you don't understand the terminology being used.

Nine key steps in the systematic review process

Table 9.4 outlines nine key steps in the systematic review process that we recommend you follow when doing a review as a Master's thesis. Most of these steps are exactly the same regardless of whether you are reviewing economic, clinical, educational, or environmental papers. However, some steps do require additional considerations and we'll discuss each step from the perspective of an economist carrying out a review of economic evaluations. We also highlight where the steps differ from those commonly used in other types of evidence synthesis.

Table 9.3 Key terms used in economic evaluations of health care interventions and programs

Key term	Definition
Cost effectiveness	Extent to which costs and health effects of an intervention or program can be regarded as providing value for money.
Discounting	Technique used to enable comparison of costs and/or benefits occurring in different years.
Incremental cost-effectiveness ratio	Summary of all changes in costs and benefits between the different interventions or programs.
Perspective	Viewpoint adopted in the economic evaluation. Examples include patient, health service and society.
Quality-adjusted life year	Outcome measure that captures both length of life and quality of life.
Sensitivity analysis	Technique used to test the robustness of economic results to uncertainty in parameters or methodologies.
Utility	Measure of well-being or benefit gained from a health care intervention or program.

Table 9.4 Key steps to consider in the systematic review process

Step 1	Performing scoping searches, identifying the review question and writing your protocol
Step 2	Literature searching
Step 3	Screening titles and abstracts
Step 4	Obtaining papers
Step 5	Selecting full-text papers
Step 6	Quality assessment
Step 7	Data extraction
Step 8	Analysis and synthesis
Step 9	Writing up and editing

Planning and managing your review

Before you rush off to work on your review, you need to take time to think about how you are going to plan your review activities from now until the day that you submit your thesis. A successful systematic reviewer learns to multi-task and work to deadlines.

During the review process, you will ask yourself a number of questions: Do I have the full-text papers of all of my included studies? What quality assessment checklist am I going to use? Shall I use Excel or Access to store my data? What is the submission date for my thesis? Do I have sufficient time to really think about the data I've extracted before I write my 'Discussion' and 'Conclusions' sections? Has my systematic review answered the research question? There are many different elements to manage during the review process and these are discussed in Chapter 10. You will also find useful information to help you to make sure that your review progresses smoothly – so don't forget to read, and then reread, this chapter!

Step 1 Performing scoping searches, identifying the review question and writing your protocol

Scoping searches

One of the first tasks we recommend that you carry out is your scoping searches. Scoping searches are the searches that you undertake when you are still pondering the precise wording of your review question – you use simple search terms and search only a selection of relevant sources of information. The results give you an idea of the quantity of economic evidence available to you before you carry out your main search. Chapters 2 and 3 provide detailed advice on how to carry out scoping searches.

The results of your scoping searches may be disappointing in that either you identify too many, or too few, relevant studies. If this is the case, we suggest that you meet with your supervisor and agree a plan of action so that you know exactly what to do if your 'main' search identifies too many or too few relevant studies. Unfortunately, it is not unusual to identify only one or two (or even zero) relevant economic studies when looking for health care-related economic evidence, especially if the focus of your search is a drug or device that has only recently been introduced to market. Your supervisor might think that not finding any studies is a valid result in itself, or might suggest that you broaden the scope of your review question so that additional economic studies can be included. Just remember, however, that to get good marks for your thesis you need to demonstrate that you have critical appraisal skills – this is difficult to do if you don't have any studies to critique. On the other hand, identifying too many studies means that your review question is too broad and if this is the case you need to think about the best way to narrow the focus of your review question (for example, by limiting your definition of population or choice of economic evaluation method).

Identifying the review question

Whatever the reason for carrying out a review of economic evaluations, you need to be certain that you are asking a question that can be answered. For example, you may be interested in whether the cancer drug pemetrexed offers value for money to the health service. Unfortunately, the question 'Is pemetrexed cost effective?' is too broad and, therefore, not easy to answer. Working through the 'who, what, how and where' questions and PICO (population, intervention, comparator and outcome) headings described in Chapter 2 will help you to formulate a review question that you can answer (see Box 9.1).

Box 9.1

Developing an answerable review question

What is the cost effectiveness of pemetrexed (INTERVENTION) versus gemcitabine (COMPARATOR) in the first-line treatment of patients with non-squamous disease in non-small cell lung cancer (POPULATION) in the UK NHS (SETTING) using data from cost–utility studies (OUTCOMES/STUDY DESIGN) published between 2000 and 2012 (TIME FRAME)?

Developing your review question can be a lengthy process and one which always benefits from discussions with others. As the review question that you want to answer becomes clear, your inclusion criteria will also become clear. As discussed in Chapter 2, your inclusion criteria describe the key characteristics that a study must have if it is to be included in your review – think carefully about population, intervention, comparator and outcomes. In addition, you might want to address issues of study design (for example, by choosing only full economic evaluations), language (for example, only searching for studies published in English) and time frame (for example, including only papers published after 2000). In systematic reviews of economic evaluations, reviewers often specify the method of the economic studies to be included in the review (for example, only include CEAs, or only include full economic evaluations). However, this is not always the case. Where the quantity of economic evidence available is limited, reviewers are less likely to restrict inclusion by economic evaluation method. Whether you do, or don't, apply any restrictions, you need to fully justify this decision in the 'Methods' section of your thesis.

It is good practice to state each of your inclusion criteria explicitly in your report; you could list them in a table alongside any exclusion criteria. Table

Table 9.5   Example of inclusion and exclusion criteria

	Inclusion criteria	Exclusion criteria
Review question: Is pemetrexed cost effective compared with gemcitabine in the treatment of patients with non-squamous, non-small cell lung cancer in the first-line setting using data from cost–utility analyses from 2000 to 2012?		
Population	Chemotherapy naive, first line, non-small cell lung cancer, non-squamous disease	
Intervention	Pemetrexed or gemcitabine	
Comparator	Any chemotherapy	
Outcomes	Cost per QALY gained	
Study design	Cost–utility analysis	Cost-minimization analysis, cost–benefit analysis, cost-effectiveness analysis, editorial, letter, poster, abstract, methodological paper, partial economic evaluations
Setting	UK National Health Service	Non-UK
Language	English language	
Time frame	2000–2012	
Review question: Are public health interventions aimed at low socio-economic groups a cost-effective use of resources?		
Population	Focus on people with low socio-economic status and/or health inequalities	
Intervention	Public health interventions	Pharmacological interventions
Comparator	Any	
Outcomes	Cost per LYG, cost per natural unit of effectiveness	
Study design	Full economic evaluations	Editorial, letter, poster, abstract, methodological paper, partial economic evaluations
Setting	Any	
Language	English language	
Time frame	1990–present day	

QALY = quality-adjusted life year; LYG = life year gained

9.5 shows two very different sets of inclusion and exclusion criteria for use in two different reviews of economic evaluations.

If you are finding it difficult to define your review question then read Chapter 2 again and make sure that you follow the key steps that are discussed in the chapter, namely: identify a topic that interests you, carry out scoping searches, focus your ideas to define the scope of your review and finalize your review question. There's no real rush, time spent developing your review question is always time well spent.

Protocol

We always encourage students to write a review protocol, no matter the topic area under review. A protocol doesn't have to be complicated or lengthy, but it should outline how you intend to search for evidence, screen and select studies, report and critically appraise findings. It must also describe any pre-planned data analyses. The time that you spend thinking about, and writing, your protocol will not be wasted. At times during the review process you may feel as though you are not making much progress, or you may feel uncertain about which task to do next. Having a clear and well thought out protocol means that, on such occasions, you can simply refer to it and take your own advice.

Step 2 Literature searching

Let's assume that you have carried out your scoping searches, refined your review question and written your protocol. You now need to think about your search strategy, that is, how you are going to search for economic evidence.

There are two key questions to consider:

- What databases do you want to search for economic evidence?
- What search terms do you want to use?

Databases

Most of the commonly searched health and social sciences electronic databases also index economics studies. Useful databases for the identification of economic evaluation papers relating to health and social sciences include: MEDLINE, EMBASE, NHS Economic Evaluation Database (NHS EED),

Health Economics Evaluation Database (HEED), Health Management Information Consortium (HMIC) and PsycINFO. Other useful databases that include economic studies are: Economics and Social Data Service, EconLit, Social Care Online, Educational Resources Information Centre (ERIC), Education-line, Current Education and Children's Services Research (CERUK) and Association of Public Health Observatories (APHO). See Chapter 3 and our website for a list of useful web addresses (www.liv.ac.uk/systematic-review-guide).

Large numbers of papers containing economic evidence are published each year and are indexed in different databases and on Internet websites. Depending on the focus of your review, you will need to choose your databases and websites carefully. For example, economic evaluations of health care interventions are found primarily in established medicine-related databases (for example, MEDLINE and EMBASE) whereas economic evaluations of public health interventions are more likely to be found on governmental and public sector websites (for example, National Institute for Health and Care Excellence (NICE) and APHO). If you have doubts about this part of your review we recommend that you turn to a librarian or information specialist for assistance.

Search terms

To make sure that you identify all relevant economic evidence, you should think about using a broad search strategy. The economic data that you are interested in may be hidden in the depths of the text rather than easy to spot in the title or abstract. Your objective is to identify all relevant economic evidence so that you can be sure that you are capturing the cost and benefit information that you need to answer your review question. Don't be too specific. We believe that it pays to be inclusive rather than exclusive when it comes to choosing economic search terms to identify studies. Performing a broad search means you'll find more papers than you would if you were to carry out a narrow search. So, for example, use the terms 'cost' or 'economic' rather than 'economic evaluation' and you will find more studies (as shown in Table 9.6). The extra time it takes you to look through the titles and abstracts of your retrieved papers is worthwhile, even if you find only one additional relevant economic study.

Table 9.6 Table of costing studies identified using different search terms

Electronic database searched: 2000-2012	Number of hits (Feb. 2013) – using 'cost' as a keyword	Number of hits (Feb. 2013) – using 'economic evaluation' as a keyword
MEDLINE (Health)	273,555	4,125
NHS EED (Economics)	11,413	835
PsycINFO (Psychology)	47,958	4,807
ERIC (Education)	32,847	7,708

You need to think carefully about the search terms that you use. For example, if you are only searching for economic evaluations based on the results of randomized controlled trials (RCTs), you probably won't pick up any economic papers that fail to mention RCT in the title or abstract (see Table 9.7) – even though the authors mention RCT in the main body of the text. Also, don't be tempted to use the abbreviation 'RCT' in your searches – on MEDLINE you will find approximately 6,000 hits using the keyword 'RCT' but nearer 352,000 when using the keywords 'randomized controlled trial'.

If you can, it is a good idea to ask a librarian or information specialist to check that the search terms you are planning to use will pick up all relevant studies. If you can't do this, then just check that your search terms are picking up the key economic studies that you have already identified from your scoping search results and through discussions with your supervisor. If your main search strategy is not picking up all of these studies it is time to rethink your search terms and re-run your searches. See Chapters 2 and 3 for further explanation regarding how to develop your search strategy and improve the accuracy of your searching.

Table 9.7 Impact of using 'too' specific search terms

Search terms used in MEDLINE (1948-)	Number of hits (search date: 19/07/12)
(gemcitabine and lung cancer and RCT and cost).mp.	2
(gemcitabine and lung cancer and randomized controlled trial and cost).mp.	13
(gemcitabine and lung cancer and cost).mp.	73

Step 3 Screening titles and abstracts

The third step in the review process is to use your inclusion and exclusion criteria to screen the titles and abstracts of the papers identified from your main searches. You need to refer to your criteria as you read through the titles and abstracts to identify the papers that are potentially eligible for inclusion in your review based on your specific criteria. Remember, you don't need to have the full-text papers in front of you at this stage, as you are only reading through titles and abstracts.

Step 4 Obtaining papers

For some students, obtaining full-text papers can be a welcome distraction but for others it is the most boring task in the world. You must try to obtain the full-text papers of all of the economic papers that you included in step 3. If you are unable to obtain a paper, you need to let your supervisor know and acknowledge this problem when writing up the limitations of your review.

Step 5 Selecting full-text papers

When selecting full-text papers for inclusion in your review, you follow the same process as you do when screening titles and abstracts. However, this time you have the full-text papers in front of you (in paper or in electronic format). The full text gives you the information you need to decide whether or not a study should be included in your review. You must check through the full-text paper of each study carefully so as to ensure that you don't miss any relevant information using your explicitly stated inclusion and exclusion criteria. Only after having done this will you be able to confidently include or exclude a paper from your review.

Step 6 Quality assessment

The next key step in your systematic review is the critical appraisal (or quality assessment) of your included studies. Not all reviewers of economic evidence quality assess their included studies. However, if you are aiming to produce the best review that you are capable of writing, then this is a step that you cannot afford to skip.

The quality of economic evaluations varies. Most economic evaluations are carried out by individuals with expertise in economics but some are conducted by clinicians or social scientists who are interested in exploring cost-effectiveness questions but do not have the necessary skill base to do this well. It is, therefore, really important that you are able to identify research that has been conducted and reported to a high standard so that you do not give equal weight to studies of variable quality.

Whether you carry out quality assessment before, after or during data extraction is a personal choice. Everyone has a preference – go ahead with the method that suits your style of working. Remember, you need to quality assess each included study and it is up to you whether you do this on paper or electronically.

There are many different quality assessment tools available for the critical appraisal of health economic evaluations and some are easier to use than others. Examples of quality assessment tools can be found on our website (www.liv. ac.uk/systematic-review-guide). The majority of available tools ask the same pertinent and probing questions. We suggest that you use a short version of a checklist by Drummond and colleagues (Drummond, O'Brien, Stoddart and Torrance, 1997). The short version of the checklist is shown in Table 9.8. As a student writing a thesis, we consider this 10-point checklist to be the most appropriate tool for you to use. If you are feeling very enthusiastic you could use the full 35-point version of this checklist (Drummond and Jefferson, 1996,

Table 9.8   Short checklist for assessing economic evaluations

Drummond et al. (1997) checklist questions
1   Was a well-defined question posed in answerable form?
2   Was a comprehensive description of the competing alternatives given (i.e., can you tell who did what to whom, where and how often)?
3   Was the effectiveness of the programs or services established?
4   Were all of the important and relevant costs and consequences for each alternative identified?
5   Were costs and consequences measured accurately in appropriate physical units?
6   Were costs and consequences valued credibly?
7   Were costs and consequences adjusted for differential timing?
8   Was an incremental analysis of costs and consequences performed?
9   Was allowance made for uncertainty in the estimates of costs and consequences?
10   Did the presentation and discussion of study results include issues of concern to users?

Source: Box 3.1, *Methods for the Economic Evaluation of Health Care Programmes* by Drummond, O'Brien, Stoddart and Torrance (1997). By permission of Oxford University Press

Drummond, et al. 1997). The questions posed in the Drummond checklist are generic and so can be used in the quality assessment of any economic evaluation, no matter the field of study. The questions will lead you to consider the elements of the economic study that are most important. Remember to allow yourself sufficient time to think through your answers.

There are also tools for assessing the quality of health economic models. The report by Philips et al. (2004) presents a useful review of guidelines for good practice in decision-analytic modelling in health technology assessment.

In an ideal world, you would be able to ask someone with sufficient time and suitable qualifications to read through the results of your quality assessment exercise to check the consistency of your judgments across your included studies. However, if you don't live in an ideal world (and who does?) then make sure you mention this issue when writing up the limitations of your review.

Finally, don't forget that there are also tools for assessing the quality of systematic reviews and it is always a good idea to review the quality of your own systematic review (see Chapter 4 for more details).

Step 7   Data extraction

Let's assume that you have just completed your quality assessment exercise. You are now getting to know your included studies and probably feel in control of your economic review. The next stage in the systematic review process is to carry out data extraction. However, before you can begin to extract data from your economic evaluations you need to design a data extraction form. We suggest that you turn to Chapter 5 and read the sections on designing and piloting data extraction forms. Chapter 5 also includes useful advice on how to efficiently extract data from studies and provides examples of well thought out data extraction tables.

The type of data that you extract from economic evaluations differs substantially from the data that you extract from other types of studies. However, the structure of most published reviews of health economic evaluations is straightforward and we suggest that you consider including the following data in your data extraction tables:

Table 1:   *Study characteristics*: study reference, identify whether full-text paper or abstract, type of study, intervention, study population, country, time period, industry affiliation

Table 2:   *Economic costs and outcomes*: study reference, type of model (if used), perspective, assumptions relating to costs, assumptions relating to outcomes

Table 3: *Cost items and data sources*: study reference, cost items and cost data sources, price year, currency, discount rate

Table 4: *Efficacy and outcomes sources*: study reference, efficacy data, efficacy data sources, outcomes, outcome data sources, discount rate

Table 5: *Cost-effectiveness results and conclusions*: study reference, total costs, total outcomes, ICERs, authors' conclusions

Table 6: *Sensitivity analysis*: study reference, summary of sensitivity analyses and results

As a student, you will probably be working independently. However, it is worth trying to find someone (suitably able) to check your extracted data for inaccuracies and/or transcription errors. This is particularly important if your included studies contain large, complex data tables. In terms of responsibility, this systematic review is your project and you must be accountable for all decisions made and tasks undertaken. One benefit of working alone is that you can be sure you have adopted the same approach to data extraction across all studies. As mentioned in Chapter 1, check with your supervisor regarding your institution's policy on working independently.

Step 8   Analysis and synthesis

When it comes to the systematic review of economic evaluations there are no established methods for data synthesis, other than narrative synthesis (see Chapter 5 for a discussion of narrative synthesis). So don't worry; it is probably not appropriate for you to perform a meta-analysis or a meta-ethnography. How you write up your narrative synthesis will depend on the information you have reported in your data tables. Your data tables often reveal that the results of your included studies are different: some studies may demonstrate that 'Intervention X is cost effective compared with intervention Y' whilst others may conclude that 'Intervention Y is cost effective compared with intervention X'. If this is a feature of your review then all that you can do in your narrative synthesis is report what you have found. You also need to acknowledge patterns (similarities and differences) in the data and in the reported ICERs.

There is no need to describe and then scrutinize each included study on its own merits; you need to spend your time thinking carefully about what the data are saying as a collective. Anderson (2010) argues that even trying to do this is wasted effort as the individual papers included in

systematic reviews of economic evaluations are often inherently different from each other and attempting to compare studies with different
perspectives, time frames and local settings is futile. Our alternative
perspective is that economic reviews, if carried out using systematic and
rigorous methods, can be just as informative and useful for decision making and student learning as any other type of systematic review. We agree
that reviews of economic evaluations usually comprise very different
studies; however, we believe that this is an important observation in
itself. The information described and critiqued within a review of economic evaluations may serve many purposes, including summarizing
what is currently known about a topic, helping to inform a policy decision, or identifying parameter values to use in an economic model or
economic evaluation. Even if your review concludes that the results of
the economic studies are too diverse to enable comparison, this can be a
useful finding in itself.

Step 9   Writing up and editing

A successful review of economic evaluations (and any other type of
review) is one that adds information to the existing knowledge base and
answers the review question posed. This may sound obvious to you, but
believe us, not all reviewers manage to write 'Discussion' and 'Conclusions' sections that succinctly summarize the available data or meaningfully interpret the results of all of the hard work that has been undertaken.
See Chapter 7 for more information about writing your discussion and
conclusions.

Reviewing the literature is mainly a technical exercise until this stage
in the review process and it is widely agreed that 'Discussion' and
'Conclusions' sections are the most difficult sections of any review to
write. As a reviewer you need to think carefully about the information
you have collected and decide whether there are enough data of sufficient quality to answer your review question. You really must take the
time to match the extracted economic data with the results of your quality assessment exercise and then meaningfully interpret what you have
found. There is no right or wrong way to do this. Planning your discussion and thinking through the key issues before putting pen to paper is
always a good way to start. The questions raised in Table 9.9 might help
you clarify and organize your ideas.

Table 9.9   Writing the 'Discussion' section of an economic review

	Key questions/issues to think about when writing the discussion
Number of studies	Are there sufficient studies to answer your review question? If there are very few published economic evaluations included in your review, then you need to discuss the possible reasons for this. Perhaps your inclusion criteria were too strict or you didn't search enough databases, or maybe your topic was out of date or too new?
Quality	Economic evaluations are often inherently flawed. It is important that you acknowledge the link between study results and study quality in your 'Discussion' section. It is misleading to report that all included studies demonstrated that intervention A was cost effective compared with intervention B if you don't mention that some of the studies didn't include all relevant costs, some overestimated benefits and others used limited perspectives.
Intervention and comparator	Do you have sufficient information about the intervention and comparator in each study to confidently compare them and draw conclusions? Do most of the studies in the review describe the same interventions and comparators with the same level of detail? Do any of the studies compare interventions with comparators that are no longer in use?
Perspective	Do all of the studies in the review adopt the same perspective? If not, is there a reason for this? Does the choice of perspective influence the results of the study? Narrow perspective/viewpoint: for example, patient. Wider perspective/viewpoint: for example, society.
Rate of discounting	No matter the discount rate used in a study, it is helpful if the authors explore the impact of using different discount rates as part of their sensitivity analyses, including using a rate of 0 per cent. Watch out for studies that only discount costs OR benefits and studies that apply different rates to costs and benefits. What is the approach taken in most of the studies and why?
Price year and currency	Are all of the resource items used in the economic evaluations from the same price year and estimated in the same currency? Probably not. You need to be aware of how different price years and currencies might affect the size of the calculated ICERs and how this might influence decision making.
QALYs	Where do the QALY estimates come from? From the general public or from a patient survey? What tools are used to derive utilities? Are the values used comparable across studies? Do you think there are better sources of utility values for this population?
ICERs	Are the estimated ICERs of a similar size? Are the results of the studies in agreement? If not, why not? What are the key drivers of the analyses? Are the drivers common to all studies? Can you make an overall judgment about whether or not the intervention is cost effective compared with the comparator(s)?
Sensitivity analysis	Do the authors address uncertainty in their analyses? What are the main sources of uncertainty in the economic evaluations? How is this uncertainty be handled?

(Continued)

Table 9.9   (Continued)

	Key questions/issues to think about when writing the discussion
Generalizability	Discussion of generalizability is paramount. Even if all of the evaluations in your review are expertly undertaken and assessed to be of excellent quality, if they are all inherently different in their approach to estimating cost effectiveness then you need to think about whether the results of the studies can be used to answer the review question. When conducting an economic review it is always possible that even studies that meet strict inclusion/exclusion criteria will fail on the test of generalizability. For example, some authors might include the costs of interventions that are not routinely used in all settings, others might employ a slightly wider definition of the patient population, whilst others might use published cost data from non-routine sources. Often this list is endless and it is crucial to describe overall results in light of issues of generalizability so that the reader is clear about the circumstances under which the results of the review are valid.

Final thoughts

Congratulations. You've made it – you have completed your review of economic evaluations. Is there a little voice in your head daring you to think about publishing your review? We hope so! Increasingly, reviews of economic evidence are being published in a wide variety of journals, not only specialist health economics journals. For example, you may come across a review of economic evaluations in a clinical journal or an economic review of housing alternatives in a health economics journal. You might also want to think about submitting an abstract of your review to a local, national or even international conference. We are of the opinion that if you have followed the advice in this book then your systematic review will pass even the highest of peer-review obstacles. Go on, put yourself (and your review) out there and get your results published.

> ## Key points to think about when writing your protocol
>
> - Present a clearly stated economic review question with as much detail as possible;
> - Be comprehensive when you outline your plans for searching for economic evidence;
> - Quality assessment tool – explain why you think the tool you will use is appropriate.

> ## What an examiner is looking for in your thesis
>
> - A clearly stated economic review question;
> - Appropriate search terms used and relevant databases searched for evidence;
> - Quality assessment of included studies;
> - Structured discussion showing how the quality of studies may influence the conclusions of the review;
> - Pertinent discussion of generalizability of results;
> - Statement relating to whether you were able to answer the review question.

Frequently Asked Questions

Question 1 Can I do a review of economic evaluations that are unrelated to health?

Yes, Health Economics is not the only branch of Economics that employs methods of economic evaluation – Environmental, Housing and Transport Economics do too.

Question 2 What if the prices/currencies used in my included studies are all from different years?

This is often the case. You must decide whether you need to compare the cost data from your included studies at a single point in time. You should think about whether this level of comparability is critical to the interpretation of the data and how converting prices/currencies to a base year might affect decision making. If you decide to convert your prices/currencies to a base year, then you can browse our website (www.liv.ac.uk/systematic-review-guide) for useful information on how to do this. Again, it is a good idea to discuss your planned approach with your supervisor.

Question 3 What do I do if the economic evaluations that I am interested in all adopt different viewpoints/perspectives?

You need to make sure that the issue of viewpoint/perspective is intelligently discussed in your thesis. It is misleading to conclude that most of the results discussed in the included studies are sufficiently similar if the analyses have been conducted from widely different viewpoints. You need to think through your findings and comment on how choice of perspective can influence the magnitude of the estimated ICERs.

Question 4 How do I make sure that the conclusions of the review are generalizable to all users?

You can't. You can only write your conclusions based on the evidence that is described in your included studies. You need to think about the question that you set out to answer and make sure that you have attempted to do this to the best of your ability based on the nature and quality of the data that are available to you.

10

Planning and Managing My Review

Gerlinde Pilkington and Juliet Hockenhull

guide
supervisor studies
searches methods outcomes economics
protocol research
practical quantitative
meta-analysis
synthesis systematic
student databases management
FAQ discussion
question post-graduate
qualitative searching review
quality-assessment
thesis data

This chapter will help you to:

- plan and make appropriate use of the resources available to you;
- co-ordinate your research activities;
- feel confident managing all aspects of the systematic review from start to finish;
- write your thesis document and submit your thesis on time.

Introduction

Chapters 2 to 7 discussed each step of the systematic review process in detail. Chapter 8 presented an overview of qualitative evidence synthesis and Chapter 9 introduced the principles of economic evidence synthesis. Having provided you with the advice that you need to understand the systematic review process, our book could end here. However, students often ask us questions about how to plan and manage reviews. We therefore decided to conclude our book with this final hands-on chapter, which is full of practical advice about planning and managing a systematic review as part of an academic thesis.

This chapter focuses on how you can co-ordinate your review activities, and suggests how you can employ the resources at your disposal to maximize the chances that the review will progress smoothly. We start by helping you to consider the key resources available to you before you start your review. We then discuss hints and tips for successful time and resource management that you can use as your review progresses. Some of the points considered in this chapter have already been addressed in other chapters, but we feel it's necessary to stress their importance once again.

Help: Where do I start?

Now that you have read this book, you should be ready to begin your journey. You may be feeling both apprehensive and excited and you may have many questions regarding the research process and be wondering what lies ahead. Be assured that you are not alone! This chapter has been designed to help by offering you advice on how to successfully manage each stage of your research project.

Don't just think of the review process as one distinct entity; break it down into bite-sized chunks – macro managing the whole journey and micro managing the individual stops along the way. Planning ahead and thinking about each stage at the outset can help save time later. Organization and planning are the key factors to successfully completing a systematic review, so take a deep breath, get out your pen and paper (or keyboard, tablet, laptop or smartphone) and get started. Put a plan in place now for the research activities you need to undertake. However, be aware that plans don't always go as intended, and as a researcher you need to learn to be pragmatic and flexible and adjust your timetable as necessary.

The first thing that you need to think about is the submission deadline for your thesis. As a student, it is likely that you will be working to a tight time schedule. Think about when your thesis is due to be submitted and plan backwards from then to now. Whether you are looking at months or weeks, you will find that the review process will expand to fill the time that you have available.

The next thing that we recommend that you do, as outlined in Chapter 2, is write a review protocol (a summary of the methods that you are planning to follow during the review process). As you will have noticed, most of the chapters in this book contain a list of points to consider when writing your review protocol. Their aim is to provide you with key information that you can use to guide the development of your review protocol. Writing a review protocol makes you think about the overall review process and therefore allows realistic goals to be set at the start of the project. It is likely that only you and your supervisor will ever read your protocol, so you don't need to worry too much about structure or style; your supervisor will prefer you to concentrate on the content. You don't have to write a protocol, but we encourage you to do so! Take a look at our website for examples of published protocols that we've used to guide our systematic reviews (www.liv.ac.uk/systematic-review-guide).

You also need to consider the potential scale of your review. For example, the results of your scoping searches should give you an idea of the volume and type of relevant studies available. If your review is likely to include a small number of studies (that is, fewer than five) then spending time setting up systems and learning new software may not be time well spent. However, if you are likely to include more than five studies in your review, then use of bibliographic software may save you time and effort in the long run. The design of your included studies also affects how you manage your review. For example, quantitative and qualitative studies are likely to require different analysis packages. Having a clear idea, from the outset, of the direction of your review allows you to investigate the available data management and analysis options.

If we liken the systematic review process to a journey, planning the route is essential. You need to know how long you have to reach your destination (when do you submit?), what type of route you are going to take (qualitative/ quantitative?) and what to pack for your journey (what resources?). The rest of this chapter focuses on how you can co-ordinate your activities, and we suggest how you can use the resources at your disposal to ensure that your review continues moving forward without too many disruptions.

What types of resources are available?

Time: As a student you will be very aware that your project has a deadline – an often inflexible one that is set by your academic institution. Careful planning, efficient project management and realistic expectations of what is achievable will enable you to make the most of your time. You will make life much easier for yourself if you overestimate, rather than underestimate, the time it takes to complete key tasks.

People: During the review process other people, for example, supervisor, co-students and/or family, may be available to contribute to review activities. These activities include cross-checking extracted data, quality assessment or proofreading text. More importantly, don't forget to call on the help of other reviewers, information specialists and/or statisticians if you need them – they can help you to choose the most effective review methods, search for evidence, locate references and analyse your data appropriately. You need to speak to your supervisor to find out how much of a contribution from others is allowed, as some academic courses demand that every piece of work that you produce is entirely your own. In our view, having somebody to assist you with, for example, study selection does not violate this principle any more than asking your supervisor for guidance.

Tools: We are assuming that, as a student, you are using a computer and have Internet access. We also assume that you are using a word-processing package to write up the different stages of your review. There is an array of tools available to help you manage your research. These include software packages that can assist with data management, data storage and structured thesis template examples. In particular, think about the advantages and disadvantages of using a bibliographic software package to manage your studies (for example, EndNote or RefWorks). Be creative. Look for technology that can help you conduct your review, chat to other students about the tools that they have used, or will be using, and listen to your supervisor's advice.

Managing your time and co-ordinating activities

Figure 10.1 lists all of the individual steps in the systematic review process that are discussed throughout this book, which hopefully are now familiar to you. It can be used as a checklist of the different stages that you will inevitably go through when completing your review. You can use it as you make plans to start your journey, building in some scheduled stops before arriving on time at your final destination.

Time is probably the most crucial resource you have so it's a good idea to plan now for what lies ahead. You need to make sure you meet your timelines,

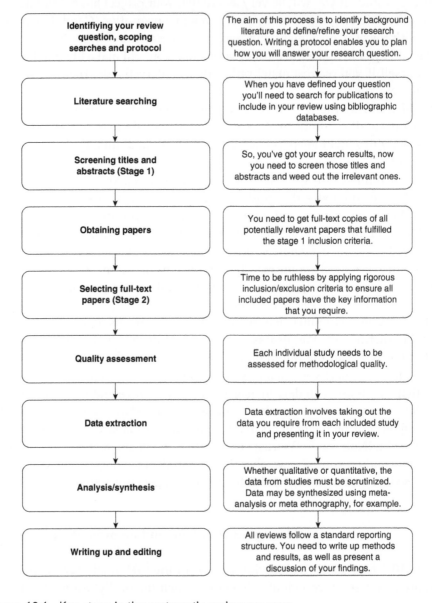

Figure 10.1 Key steps in the systematic review process

whether self-imposed or supervisor-driven. Start by managing your review project as you mean to go on. Be calm, organized and efficient. Unfortunately, we can't tell you how much time to allocate to the individual stages of your review. Each review (and reviewer) is different and, with so many unforeseeable factors at play, the best advice we can give you is that, inevitably, some deadlines will be missed. Just make sure that know your final submission deadline and that it is met.

When it comes to systematic reviewing, you will never find that you have spare time on your hands – even if you might want (need) some. While some tasks may seem tedious (or perhaps you may just put off doing a task because you don't think you have time to complete it before you have to go out), you can always find a different task to be getting on with. You'll soon learn that you can start a task and then put it on hold whilst you make progress with another task. As you get on with your review you will be working on distinct, yet overlapping, activities. You might find that while some tasks are ongoing (such as waiting for the arrival of the full-text papers that you have ordered) you can get on with something else (such as reading the papers that you already have).

Peers, friends and/or family are often quite willing to help out with some basic tasks. For example, during screening and applying inclusion criteria, your supervisor or peer could cross-check a random sample (say 10 per cent) of your decisions. This helps to ensure you are not dismissing potentially relevant studies. From an editing perspective, your supervisor should take a periodic look at drafts of your work and provide feedback. How this will be done, and when, needs to be negotiated in advance with your supervisor to ensure that you are both aware of when you will send drafts and receive feedback. We all have friends and family who are great at spotting mistakes; you can ask them to read chapters of your work and to do their best to find typing errors or half-written sentences. Just make sure you (and your collaborator(s)) are clear on expectations and timelines before you begin.

Another way to make best use of your time is to make sure that your work, from initial drafting of your protocol to final editing of your thesis, is consistent. Establishing consistency across all aspects of the review process early on can save precious time and effort later. You might wonder why this is important at such an early stage and perhaps you are thinking, 'Surely I can go back and change minor things later?' The short answer to this is that 'minor' things can end up as 'major' things. It is likely that you will end up spending hours and hours editing sections of text in your document because you didn't carefully consider consistency (in formatting, data extraction, analysis and so on) at the beginning of your research. We suggest that you consider the following advice as you conduct your review:

- Throughout your project, be consistent with use of terminology. For example, some authors will discuss health status, treatments and patient groups, whilst other authors will talk about health outcomes, interventions and populations. You need to choose the terms that you want to use and stick with them.
- Think carefully before using abbreviations, but if you have to use an abbreviation then be consistent. For example, if you want to abbreviate the phrase 'cardiovascular disease' don't use both CD and CVD.
- Always list the included studies in your tables in the same way (alphabetically or chronologically) – just be consistent throughout your document.

Managing your review: employing the right resources for the job

Now that we've discussed time-saving tips and highlighted potential pitfalls, it's time to consider how other resources can be used to make the review process easier for you to manage.

Managing your record keeping

Make record keeping a priority! Record keeping is a basic and required step in project management and allows you to keep an up-to-date and accurate account of what you have done at different stages of the review. It also helps you to outline and plan future activities. Unfortunately, it is an activity that is all too often neglected during the review process. Inevitably, the reviewer ends up questioning his/her own actions: Why did I leave out that study? Did I search that database? How many duplicate references did I have? The best way to avoid such unnecessary stress is to take note of everything you do as you carry out day-to-day review activities. There are many ways to keep records, from paper and pen notes written chronologically to the use of electronic database systems tailored to suit your review. Choose the method that you prefer. From our experience, electronic record keeping is more efficient than the pen and paper method, especially when it comes to searching for information, and it is satisfyingly time-saving if you are dealing with a large number of included studies.

Table 10.1 gives an example of record keeping. Keeping thorough and accurate records in this way allows you to review the decisions you have made and having the information to hand can help you to defend and justify your decision making. For example, if you are asked why a specific paper was not included

Table 10.1 Example of record keeping

Reference	Included at screening?	Obtained paper	Included at selection?	Reason for exclusion
Anderton (2002)	Yes	Electronic	No	Inappropriate population
Apple (2013)	Yes	Paper	Yes	Not applicable
Brent (2002)	Yes	Still to get		
Bryan (2002)	No	Not needed		Inappropriate intervention
Clyde (2003)	Yes	PDF	Yes	Not applicable

in your review, you can easily check your records and determine whether it was included in your search results and, if it was, the reason for its subsequent exclusion. We've included example tables on our website (www.liv.ac.uk/systematic-review-guide), so take your pick.

In addition, we suggest that you keep a research activity journal (again, electronic or paper) on a daily or weekly (as appropriate) basis. The purpose of this journal is to allow you to look back and reflect, at regular intervals, on your more general research activities. This will enable you to monitor progress and highlight issues that you might want to return to at a later date.

Managing your files (paper or electronic)

The term 'managing files' (electronic and/or paper) relates to systems for storing information, backing up information and keeping files in order so that you are always working on the most up-to-date version of your document.

Storing information

During the review process, organized storage of information is essential. The storage of information is comparable to packing for a journey; you need to have more than enough space in your car as you know that you will be picking up more passengers along the way.

However small you think your project is, you will soon be engulfed in piles of papers, information, data and different versions of reports and tables. Before you even start your review you need to think about how you will keep track and store your electronic and non-electronic data. Clearly ordered information storage systems accompanied by good record keeping and unique labelling of studies will help you to quickly access information as and when required by your review.

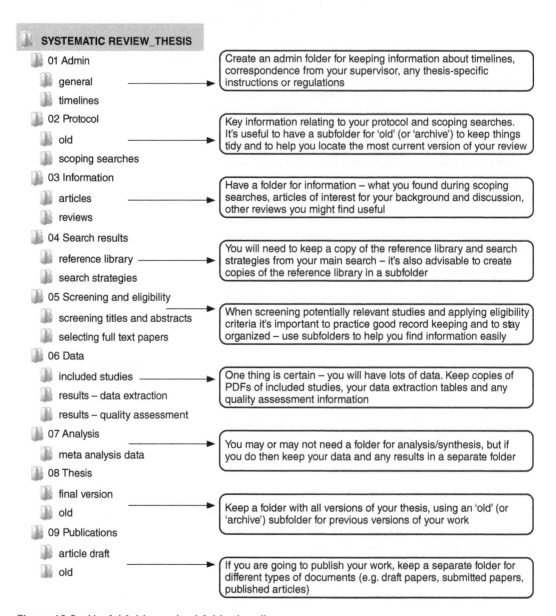

Figure 10.2   Useful folder and subfolder headings

When storing files electronically, the use of folders and subfolders can be a considerable help. It is a good idea to set up folders to allow you to save files in a logical manner. An example of how to organize all the information and data you might gather during the review process is shown in Figure 10.2.

This is by no means exhaustive, and perhaps small reviews might adopt a simpler system. Note how many of the folders and subfolders match with the key stages of the review process shown in Figure 10.1.

Backing up information

The ideal electronic system has automatic, built-in backup facilities but if this isn't a feature of your computer, make sure you back up your work regularly. You could use a removable memory stick, external hard drive, or web-based storage to keep copies – get into good habits early on and it will save you time and effort later in the review. For example, make sure that, on a regular basis, you back up your work to your computer, leave an electronic copy with a friend or colleague, send the latest version to yourself via email as well as backing up to your academic institution's file storage. This might sound a little excessive but you can never have too many backups!

Keeping files in order

You also need to consider version control. You need to make sure that you are always working on the most up to date copy of your work, be it data extraction tables, report writing, or use of references. One way of managing this is to include the date in the name of a file (for example, introduction_25_nov_2013). It is then important to change the date with each substantive update of your work. As can be seen in Figure 10.2, to avoid confusion older versions of your files can be moved into an archive folder.

Unique labelling of studies used in your thesis (for example, as part of background information or included studies) should be assigned consistently. For example, use of first author and year of publication (for example, Smith_2012) is a simple way to identify studies and is easy to remember; if the author has published multiple studies in a single year, include the journal title as well (for example, Smith_BMJ_2012) or add 'a', 'b', and so on to the year (for example, Smith_2012a).

Managing your data extraction

Planning how you are going to manage your data is critical to the quality of your review; it is important that you are clear about the data you need, how you are going to use the data and what format the data need to be in. Furthermore, you need to know all of this before you begin to extract data from your included studies.

Not all study authors will report the data that interest you in the same way. You need to try to make the data that you are extracting as uniform as possible so that it can be used as planned when it comes to data analysis and synthesis. For example, when data extracting participant characteristics, authors can choose to record age as a mean value (65 years of age), median value (62 years of age) or present a range of ages (58 to 70 years of age). For your review, you should extract data on participant age in such a way that you can compare age across your included studies. Designing and piloting a structured data extraction form and thinking carefully about how each required field should be completed (and therefore reported in your thesis) will go a long way to ensuring that the data that you have extracted can be used as you had originally planned. The content of the data extraction form must always be considered in relation to the reporting tables that you plan to use in your thesis (for example, participant characteristics, study characteristics and study results).

Managing your references

We recommend that students use some form of bibliographic software package to facilitate storage and use of references. If you do not have access to such a program through your academic institution there are several open access (free) programs available on the Internet.

The main purpose of bibliographic software is to help you to organize, annotate and integrate required references into your work. As a systematic reviewer, this type of software offers you the following benefits:

- Automatic download of reference details (titles, abstracts, keywords, etc.) from electronic databases (for example, Web of Knowledge);
- Electronic storage of all reference information, including notes, images and PDFs;
- Ability to group and organize studies using keywords (for example, background, included studies, excluded studies);
- The function of adding and formatting in-text citations and bibliographies (for example, Harvard or Vancouver style).

Although extremely useful, bibliographic software is not infallible. It is necessary to check that automatically downloaded references have been imported correctly from each electronic database. It is also important to check for spelling mistakes and capitalization, particularly if you have entered references by hand, and that in-text citations and bibliographies are formatted correctly. Remember, if you are manually typing references into your reference library, each field (such as 'journal title' or 'authors') may have to be entered in a specific way.

It is worth noting that examiners often check the accuracy of the referencing in a thesis to allow them to form an overall assessment of the student's attention to detail. Bibliographic software, appropriately used, helps you to make a good impression without having to make too much effort.

Practical applications: choosing the right software

Table 10.2 lists different types of software packages that you might think about using during your systematic review. It gives practical advice on how and when you might use these packages. The accompanying pros and cons will help you to make an informed choice when it comes to identifying the most appropriate software packages. The right tools for the right job make everything go smoother – why walk to the next town when you can hitch a ride with a friend?

Writing your thesis document

You will need to obtain (and follow) a copy of your academic institution's thesis submission guidelines. Read this document thorughly, boring as this may be, before you even begin your systematic review. Key things to look for are: required thesis structure, length and recommended referencing system. What we present here stems from our experiences of building documents that require consistent presentation of text, headings, tables, figures and references. Remember, word-processing packages make it easy for you when it comes to writing up your thesis. Not only do they have set styles for headings, subheadings, regular text and bullet lists, they can even create your table of contents. As you become familiar with the software you will find all sorts of helpful features that will allow you to manage your review efficiently and effectively. Don't forget to make full use of the search facility

Table 10.2 Software packages available and their pros and cons

Software package	What can I do with it?	Advantages	Disadvantages
Word-processing software	Keep records of: Time management Progress made Search results Reference lists and unique identifiers Which studies are included Create forms for: Inclusion/exclusion Data extraction Quality assessment Writing up and editing Also: Create templates and use pre-set styles	A word-processing package is very useful for all stages of the review, not just writing up. You will be able to look back and reflect on decisions made – justification and accountability are crucial in a viva voce situation.	Compared with spreadsheets and database software, word-processing packages have less functionality when it comes to creating and manipulating tables. Additionally, they are not always the best choice when dealing with complex numeric data – they are more suited to text.
Spreadsheet software	Keep records of: Time management Progress made Reference lists and unique identifiers Which studies are included Create forms for: Inclusion/exclusion Data extraction Quality assessment Manipulation of numerical data Also: Create tables, graphs and charts	Excellent for numeric data and can be used throughout the review process. Better than a word-processing package for creating tables through use of filter and sort tools. Each workbook can contain multiple sheets. Most packages have a function which allows data to be imported and exported (for example, into a word-processing or statistical package), the same data can then be presented in different formats.	Not so useful if the majority of data is qualitative in nature. Make sure you know the basics before setting something up. Spreadsheets are often misused or data input incorrectly into inconsistently formatted cells. This can alter values and skew results.

Software package	What can I do with it?	Advantages	Disadvantages
Database software	Keep records of: Time management Progress made Search results Reference lists and unique identifiers Which studies are included Create forms for: Inclusion/exclusion Data extraction Quality assessment Also: Create tables, charts and graphs	Excellent for use in reviews with vast quantities of data. Can be used for everything other than statistical analysis, referencing and writing up your report. Databases are usually intuitive and user friendly with lots of useful functions. Each database has the capability to store multiple forms and tables which can be interlinked, and this avoids having several documents clogging up your folders. Most packages have the function to import/export data (for example, to word-processor, spreadsheet or statistical package), which enables the same data to be presented in different formats and ensures that the data are input accurately.	If you have never used a database before you might find it time consuming to learn. If you've fewer than five studies included then setting up a database probably isn't worthwhile. A few hours spent learning how to get the best from software is time well spent in a bigger or more complex review.
Specialist software (for example, statistical, qualitative)	Conduct statistical analyses Directly extract data into the package Create graphs and charts Code data Prepare data for analysis	Can perform analyses for you and produce graphs, tables and figures.	If you don't know very much about statistics then you might be analyzing your data inappropriately. If you are keen to use a statistical package then we suggest you take some time to look at the different packages available and, in consultation with an expert, decide how you might utilize them. It can take a significant period of time to learn how to use specialist packages.

(Continued)

Table 10.2 (Continued)

Software package	What can I do with it?	Advantages	Disadvantages
Reviewing software	Conduct all stages of the review using just one package	RevMan is freely available through the Cochrane Library and covers all aspects and stages of the review from the results of searching to final report writing, including production of forest plots. Even if your review is not in the style of a Cochrane review there may still be features of this system that are useful to your review.	There is less flexibility than with a complete package.
Bibliographic software	Store references De-duplicate multiple references Generate unique identifier for individual studies Use custom fields and grouping feature Insert references in-text and create bibliographies Attach PDFs and images to the correct reference	Most online databases allow you to save citations to a bibliographic software package. Use this software to create bibliographies and insert the correct references into a document – this function can save a significant amount of time. Multiple fields allow for adding notes, grouping and organizing references (that is, background, included studies, excluded studies).	Software may not be freely available via your institution; however, you can access free/online versions. It can be time consuming to learn to use. However, the likelihood is that you will spend more time referencing manually. It's a good idea to take this opportunity to learn how to use bibliographic software packages if you plan to continue in academia. Check that the word-processing package and bibliographic software that you choose are compatible.

and the electronic thesaurus. Take time to 'play' around with the programs you have chosen and discover the useful functions they offer.

Write as you go along, or at the very least keep bullet points for expansion later. We suggest that you structure your thesis as soon as you can so that you can write the straightforward sections, such as background information or research rationale, long before you start to write up your results. For information we have included a suggested thesis document structure (Box 10.1). This structure has generic headings that you might find helpful as you plan how to write up your review as your postgraduate thesis. It would also be useful to look at other published systematic reviews or theses for inspiration.

Box 10.1

Suggested thesis document structure

- Title page and preface (don't forget to include your name, date and acknowledgments, etc.)
- Glossary and definitions
- Table of contents
- Abstract or summary (a brief synopsis of all included chapters)
- Background
- Aims and objectives
- Methods
- Results
- Discussion (including principal findings, strengths and limitations, and relevant factors)
- Conclusion
- References
- Appendices

Importantly, it's all an issue of style. Does your institution have a set format for word-processed documents? Will you lose marks if you use the wrong style? For example, you could be asked to write using the Times New Roman typeface with the font size at 11pts and the spacing set to double, perhaps with a large margin. Does your subject area or institution have preferred styles of writing? Can you use abbreviations? How should you reference? We always recommend starting as you mean to go on by using the correct styles from day one.

As soon as you start to write up your review you will realize that it is extremely important for you to manage your references appropriately. You could find yourself writing text such as 'Three studies were set in Japan' or '16 studies used valid outcome measures'. You need to make sure that the reader can identify the studies to which you refer. To do this you need to add references. In this book we have not always included references when using illustrative or suggested text. However, you must! You need to plan ahead and think about how to make your review easy to read. Take, for example, the sentence: 'Three studies were set in Japan'. Using Vancouver formatting, this sentence would look like this: 'Three studies[1,2,6] were set in Japan.' Using Harvard formatting, the same sentence would look like this: 'Three studies (Brown, 1999; Smith 2000; Jones 2012) were set in Japan.' Some reference formats are more conducive than others to the reporting of systematic reviews. However, you must follow the reporting guidelines set by your institution.

Also, as we mentioned in Chapter 4, don't forget that you can use a systematic review quality assessment checklist on your own review. Using a checklist is a win–win situation – you can identify areas where your thesis is weak (and you can make changes before submission) or, more likely, you can reassure yourself that you have done a good job.

Final thoughts

So, now you have a better idea about how to make use of your time and how to co-ordinate your research activities, using the appropriate resources for each job. But we know that you're a beginner, and that this all might still seem very bewildering. We think it is a good idea for you to keep the lessons you've learnt from this chapter at the back of your mind as you work through your review – treat this chapter as a practical guide that you have to hand.

Here are our key messages:

- Organization is key to a successful review. Plan ahead but be prepared to be flexible;
- Identify the resources you have available to you;
- Plan your file storage system at the beginning of the project so you know where information is to be stored;
- Back up files regularly;
- Keep detailed records of the tasks that you've done;
- Use a bibliographic software package;
- Check institution style guides for thesis submission;
- Larger or more complex reviews may benefit from the use of specialist software packages;
- Speak to supervisors and/or experts for help and advice.

Key points to consider when writing your protocol

- Well-designed protocols reflect most of the headings in Box 10.1 with the exception of results and discussion. Protocols usually include a section on project timelines – use the information in this chapter to help plan your time.

What an examiner is looking for in your thesis

- A well-structured document that adheres to institutional submission guidelines;
- Academic style with appropriate use of language and with no (or very few) spelling mistakes and typing errors – if this is an area where you are weak, for example if English is not your first language, then seek assistance;
- Appropriately formatted (and correct) references and similarly correct reference list – don't throw away marks by skimping on this aspect of your thesis.

Frequently Asked Questions

Question 1 As well as studying I work full time, so how can I manage my time?

Many of the tasks, such as scan-reading and data extraction, can be carried out in short time slots. Make the most of the time that you do have available. For example, if you have an hour free, scan-read some titles. An important thing to remember is that, with certain non-critical tests, it is OK to start a new task before you have completed an old one. Be flexible, co-ordinate your activities to reflect the time available on any given day, but remember that you will need to block out some dedicated time for writing up.

Question 2 What do I do if an article that I ordered arrives later than planned?

It depends. If the article arrives on the day that you are due to submit your thesis, then you can acknowledge its existence without incorporating it into your review. You might state, 'The following study was received too late for incorporation in the review. However, future updates should examine its eligibility and implications.' If it arrives the week before you are due to submit, and you are confident that inclusion will not change your conclusions, you could state, 'The following study was received too late for incorporation in the review; however, a cursory examination suggests that the results of the current review would not be sensitive to its findings.' If it arrives the week before you are due to submit, and you believe that inclusion will change your review findings, then you need to discuss what to do about it with your supervisor and make a pragmatic decision based on what you can realistically achieve during the week before submission.

Question 3   I don't know what to do about the statistical aspects of my review – what are statistical software packages, and will they help me?

Statistical software packages are specialized computer programs for combining numerical data. It is possible that, at some point in your review, you will need to use a statistical package to conduct statistical analyses and/or produce graphs and tables. If you are not familiar with statistical software packages then you are probably not very familiar with statistics either. This means that you really should get statistical advice from an expert.

Question 4   Should I use a spreadsheet (for example, Excel) or a database (for example, Access)?

The tasks that can be achieved using spreadsheets and databases are similar – both systems use tables to store data. However, whilst there is an overlap in functionality, they are designed to carry out different jobs. In short, spreadsheets are essentially large tables (or several tables) that have the ability to run formulae, analyse and produce summaries and reports of data. Databases are large tables which can store vast amounts of data in various formats; tables can be interlinked and manipulated. There isn't a right or wrong choice; your choice will be based on what software you think best fits the needs of your review.

Epilogue

Well, you are nearing the end of your systematic review journey. We hope that the experience of completing your review has been both educational and, dare we say, enjoyable. For some of you, submission and approval of your thesis may feel like the final destination. It is a significant achievement and you should be proud of attaining a new academic standing. However, we don't think that your journey should end with the submission of your thesis. We tell students that if we were in charge, all postgraduate students carrying out a systematic review for their thesis would be required to at least think about disseminating their review to an audience wider than that of their supervisor(s) and examiner(s). We would also ask them to include in an appendix of their thesis a draft paper for submission to a journal. Of course, students are *very* pleased that we do not have the power to enforce this.

However, we do think that you should consider how the results of your review could be disseminated. It may be that you can use the conclusions of your review to implement changes in your professional practice and/or it might encourage you to conduct further research. You might even want to consider presenting your work at a conference – local, national or international. We find that students are hesitant to take this next logical and, it might be said, ethical step. However, we do not think they should be hesitant. We have seen the completion of numerous systematic reviews, many with the potential to make a valuable contribution in their given fields, but their results were not disseminated.

The most common reasons given by students for not publishing their reviews are that they do not consider their review to be of a sufficiently high standard or that they do not feel 'qualified' to disseminate the results. However, if your supervisor, academic or professional colleagues are encouraging you to publish, please do not dismiss them out of hand. Remember, your supervisor is best placed to recognize the contribution that publishing your research might make to the professional practice of others and is the best person to offer you advice on how to publish your systematic review.

Whatever decision you make, we wish you well. We hope that this book has helped you to successfully complete your systematic review and that you will put your newly acquired research skills to good use.

Suggestions for further reading

If you are interested in further reading, please see the following excellent texts:

Aveyard, H. (2010) *Doing a Literature Review in Health and Social Care: A Practical Guide*. Maidenhead, Berkshire: Open University Press.

Bettany-Saltikov, J. (2012) *How To Do a Systematic Review in Nursing: A Step by Step Guide*. Maidenhead, Berkshire: Open University Press.

Booth, A., Papaioannou, D. and Sutton, A. (2011) *Systematic Approaches to a Successful Literature Review*. London: SAGE.

Gough, D., Oliver, S. and Thomas, J. (eds) (2012) *An Introduction to Systematic Reviews*. London: SAGE.

Institute of Medicine (U.S.) Committee on Standards for Systematic Reviews of Comparative Effectiveness Research, Eden, J. and Levit, L. (eds) (2011) *Finding what Works in Health Care: Standards for Systematic Reviews*. Washington, DC: The National Academies Press.

Petticrew, M. and Roberts, H. (2005) *Systematic Reviews in the Social Sciences*. Oxford: Blackwell.

References

Altman, D. (1991) *Practical Statistics for Medical Research*. London: Chapman and Hall.

American Educational Research Association (2013) Standards for Reporting on Empirical Social Science Research in AERA Publications. Available from: www.aera.net/ResearchPolicyAdvocacy/AERAShapingResearchPolicy/tabid/10297/Default.aspx (January 2013).

Anderson, R. (2010) Systematic reviews of economic evaluations: utility or futility? *Health Economics,* 19(3), 350–64.

British Library Archives (2013) The British newspaper archives. Available from: www.bl.uk/ (February 2013).

Brown, T., Pilkington, G., Bagust, A., Boland, A., Oyee, J., Tudur-Smith, C., Blundell, M., Lai, M., Martin Saborido, C., Greenhalgh, J., Dundar, Y. and Dickson R. (2013) Clinical effectiveness and cost-effectiveness of first-line chemotherapy for adult patients with locally advanced or metastatic non-small cell lung cancer: A systematic review and economic evaluation. *Health Technology Assessment,* 17(31):1–278.

The Campbell Collaboration (2012) The Campbell Collaboration. Available from: www.campbellcollaboration.org (October 2012).

CASP (2013) Critical Appraisal Skills Program: Making sense of evidence. Available from: www.casp-uk.net/ (January 2013).

Centre for Reviews and Dissemination (2009) Systematic reviews: CRD's guidance for undertaking reviews in healthcare. Available from: www.york.ac.uk/inst/crd/SysRev/!SSL!/WebHelp/SysRev3.htm (January 2013).

Chalmers, I., Enkin, M. and Keirse, M. (eds) (1989) *Effective Care in Pregnancy and Childbirth*. Oxford: Oxford University Press.

Chalmers, I., Hedges, L. V. and Cooper, H. (2002) A brief history of research synthesis. *Evaluation and the Health Professions,* 25(1), 12–37.

Chalmers, I., Hetherington, J., Newdick, M., Mutch, L., Grant, A., Enkin, M., Enkin, E. and Dickersin, K. (1986) The Oxford Database of Perinatal Trials: Developing a register of published reports of controlled trials. *Journal of Controlled Clinical Trials,* 7(4), 306–24.

Cherry, M.G. (2013) *Exploring the relationships between attachment style, emotional intelligence and patient-provider communication*. PhD thesis, University of Liverpool.

Cochrane, A.L. (1972) *Effectiveness and Efficiency: Random Reflections on Health Services*. London: Nuffield Provincial Hospitals Trust.

Cochrane, A.L. (1979) *1931–1971: A critical review. Medicines for the Year 2000.* London: Office of Health Economics.

Cohen, J. (1988) *Statistical Power Analysis in the Behavioral Sciences* (2nd ed.). Hillsdale, NJ: Lawrence Erlbaum Associates, Inc.

Cooper, H. (2010) *Research Synthesis and Meta-Analysis: A Step-by-Step Approach.* London: SAGE.

Cowley, D.E. (1995) Prostheses for primary total hip replacement: A critical appraisal of the literature. *International Journal of Technology Assessment in Health Care*, 11, 770–8.

Deeks, J., Dinnes, J., D'Amico, R., Sowden, A., Sakarovitch, C., Song, F., Petticrew, M., Altman, D.G., International Stroke Trial Intervention Group and European Carotid Surgery Trial Collaborative Group (2003) Evaluating non-randomised intervention studies. *Health Technology Assessment*, 7(27), 1–173.

Department for International Development (2012) Systematic reviews in international development: An initiative to strengthen evidence-informed policy making. Available from: www.dfid.gov.uk/what-we-do/research-and-evidence/case-studies/research-case-studies/2011/systematic-reviews-background/ (October 2012).

Downs, S.H. and Black, N. (1998) The feasibility of creating a checklist for the assessment of the methodological quality of both randomised and non-randomised studies of health care interventions. *Journal of Epidemiology and Community Health*, 52, 337–84.

Drummond, M. and Jefferson, T. (1996) Guidelines for authors and peer reviewers of economic submissions to the BMJ: The BMJ Economic Evaluation Working Party. *British Medical Journal*, 313(7052), 275–83.

Drummond, M., O'Brien, B., Stoddart, G. and Torrance, G. (1997) *Methods for the Economic Evaluation of Health Care Programs.* Oxford: Oxford University Press.

Economic and Social Research Council (2013) Economic and Social Research Council: Research catalogue. Available from: www.esrcsocietytoday.ac.uk/impacts-and-findings/research-catalogue/index.aspx (February 2013).

Egger, M., Smith, G. and Altman, D. (2001) *Systematic Reviews in Health Care: Meta-Analysis in Context* (2nd ed.). London: British Medical Journal Books.

EQUATOR (2013) EQUATOR Network website. Available from www.equator-network.org/home/ (January 2013).

Fleeman, N., Bagust, A., Boland, A., Dickson, R., Dundar, Y., Moonan, M., Oyee, J., Blundell, M., Davis, H., Armstrong, A. and Thorp, N. (2011) Lapatinib and trastuzumab in combination with an aromatase inhibitor for the first-line treatment of metastatic hormone receptor positive breast cancer which over-expresses human epidermal growth factor 2 (HER2): A systematic review and economic analysis. *Health Technology Assessment*, 15(42), 1–93.

Flemming, K. and Briggs, M. (2007) Electronic searching to locate qualitative research: Evaluation of three strategies. *Journal of Advanced Nursing*, 57, 95–100.

Glass, G.V. (1976) Primary, secondary, and meta-analysis of research. *Educational Researcher*, 5(10), 3–8.

Greenhalgh, J., Bagust, A., Boland, A., Martin Saborido, C., Oyee, J., Blundell, M., Dundar, Y., Dickson, R., Proudlove, C. and Fisher, M. (2011) Clopidogrel and modified-release dipyridamole for the prevention of occlusive vascular events (review of Technology Appraisal No. 90): A systematic review and economic analysis. *Health Technology Assessment,* 15(31), 1–178.

Greenhalgh, J., Dickson, R. and Dundar, Y. (2009) The effects of biofeedback for the treatment of essential hypertension: A systematic review. *Health Technology Assessment,* 13(46), 1–104.

Higgins, J. and Green, S. (2011) Cochrane Handbook for Systematic Reviews of Interventions. Available from: www.cochrane-handbook.org (June 2013).

Joanna Briggs Institute (2011) Reviewers' Manual. Available from: www.joanna-briggs.edu.au (June 2013).

Khan, K., Kunz, R., Kleijnen, J. and Antes, G. (2003) *Systematic Reviews to Support Evidence-Based Medicine: How to Review and Apply Findings of Healthcare Research.* London: Royal Society of Medicine Press.

Liberati, A., Altman, D.G., Tetzlaff, J., Mulrow, C., Gøtzsche, P.C, Ioannidis, J.P.A., Clarke, M., Devereaux, P.J, Kleijnen, J. and Moher, D. (2009) The PRISMA statement for reporting systematic reviews and meta-analyses of studies that evaluate healthcare interventions: Explanation and elaboration. *British Medical Journal,* 339, b2535.

Library of Congress (2013) Chronicling America – historic American newspapers. Available from: http://chroniclingamerica.loc.gov/ (February 2013).

Moher, D., Liberati, A., Tetzlaff, J. and Altman, D.G. (2009) Preferred reporting items for systematic reviews and meta-analyses: The PRISMA statement. *British Medical Journal,* 339, b2535.

Mullins, G. and Kiley, M. (2002) 'It's a PhD, not a Nobel Prize': How experienced examiners assess research theses. *Studies in Higher Education,* 27(4), 369–86.

National Institute for Health and Clinical Excellence (2009) Methods for the Development of NICE Public Health Guidance (2nd ed.). Available from: www.nice.org.uk/media/CE1/F7/CPHE_Methods_manual_LR.pdf (December 2012).

Noyes, J. and Lewin, S. (2011) Supplemental guidance on selecting a method of qualitative evidence synthesis and integrating qualitative evidence with Cochrane Intervention Reviews, Chapter 6 in Noyes. J., Booth, A., Hannes, K., Harden, A., Harris, J., Lewin, S. and Lockwood, C. (eds) *Supplementary Guidance for Inclusion of Qualitative Research in Cochrane Systematic Reviews of Interventions.* Version 1 (updated August 2011). Cochrane Collaboration Qualitative Methods Group. Available from: http://cqrmg.cochrane.org/supplemental-handbook-guidance (June 2013).

Philips, Z., Ginnelly, L., Sculpher, M., Claxton, K., Golder, S., Riemsma, R., Woolacott, N. and Glanville, J. (2004) Review of guidelines for good practice in decision-analytic modelling in health technology assessment. *Health Technology Assessment,* 8(36), 1–158.

Pope, D.P., Mishra, V., Thompson, L., Siddiqui, A.R., Rehfuess, E.A., Weber, M. and Bruce, N.G. (2010) Risk of low birth weight and stillbirth associated with indoor air pollution from solid fuel use in developing countries. *Epidemiologic Reviews,* 32(1), 70–81.

Reisch, J., Tyson, J.E. and Mize, S. G. (1989) Aid to the evaluation of therapeutic studies. *Pediatrics,* 84: 815–27.

Ring, N., Ritchie, K., Mandava, L. and Jepson, R. (2011) A guide to synthesising qualitative research for researchers undertaking health technology assessments and systematic reviews. Available from: www.healthcareimprovementscotland.org/programmes/clinical__cost_effectiveness/programme_resources/synth_qualitative_research.aspx (September 2012).

Saborido, C.M., Hockenhull, J., Bagust, A., Boland, A. and Dickson, R. (2010) Systematic review and cost-effectiveness evaluation of 'pill-in-the-pocket' strategy for paroxysmal atrial fibrillation compared to episodic in-hospital treatment or continuous antiarrhythmic drug therapy. *Health Technology Assessment*, 14(31), 1–75.

Sandelowski, M., Barroso, J. and Voils, C. (2007) Using qualitative metasummary to synthesize qualitative and quantitative descriptive findings. *Research in Nursing and Health*, 3(1), 99–111.

Social Care Institute for Excellence (2010) SCIE systematic research reviews: Guidelines. Available from: www.scie.org.uk/publications/researchresources/rr01.pdf (February 2013).

The Cochrane Collaboration (2012) The Cochrane Collaboration. Available from: www.cochrane.org/ (October 2012).

Thomas, H. (no date) Quality assessment tool for quantative studies. Effective Public Health Practice Project. McMaster University: Toronto.

Tong, A., Flemming, K., McInnes, E., Oliver, S. and Craig, J. (2012) Enhancing transparency in reporting the synthesis of qualitative research: ENTREQ. *BMC Medical Research Methodology*, 12, 181.

US National Institutes of Health (2013) ClinicalTrials.gov. Available from: http://clinicaltrials.gov/ (February 2013).

US National Library of Medicine (2013) Medical Subject Headings. Available from: www.nlm.nih.gov/mesh/meshhome.html (January 2013).

Wells, G., Shea, B., O'Connell, D., Peterson, J., Welch, V., Losos, M. and Tugwell, P. (2012) The Newcastle–Ottawa Scale (NOS) for assessing the quality of nonrandomised studies in meta-analyses. Available from: www.ohri.ca/programs/clinical_epidemiology/oxford.asp (January 2013).

Zaza, S., Wright-de Aguero, L.K., Briss, P.A., Truman, B.I., Hopkins, D.P., Hennessy, M.H, Sosin, D.M., Anderson, L., Carande-Kulis, V.G., Teutsch, S.M. and Pappaioanou, M. (2000) Data collection instrument and procedure for systematic reviews in the Guide to Community Preventive Services. *American Journal of Preventative Medicine*, 18(1), 44–74.

Index

Note: Page numbers in *italic* refer to tables and figures.